D1228543

Perseverance

How a Determined Athlete Tenaciously Overcame a Stroke

by

Marie Bartoletti

ISBN: 978-1-935802-42-6

Cover illustration provided by Ella Buffo, a student in Marie's fifth grade class at McClellan Elementary School.

FATHER&SON
PUBLISHING, INC.

4909 North Monroe Street
Tallahassee, Florida 32303

Printed in China

Foreword

"*Someone in the United States has a stroke every 40 seconds. Every 4 minutes, someone dies of stroke.*" Benjamin EJ, Blaha MJ, Chiuve SE, et al. on behalf of the American Heart Association Statistics Committee and Stroke Statistics Subcommittee.

I have the honor of knowing one of the survivors, Marie Bartoletti. She came to Crossroads Speech and Hearing, Inc. following a stroke that impacted her ability to communicate. As her Speech Pathologist, it's my role to provide activities and strategies to assist patients with their struggle in finding their words, describing how they feel or what they need, or have difficulty forming the words in their mouth. Stroke is life altering. Patients go from their daily routine to various degrees of deficits and frustration following a stroke.

Marie is a determined individual. Be it a marathon, teaching a class, or any aspect of her life, she gives it her all. Her determined nature has helped her throughout the stroke rehabilitation process. And it is a process! Throughout the years, Marie had heard from many acquaintances that she should write a book. What started off as a therapeutic activity in our speech therapy sessions has become the book you are about to read. It is Marie's determination that lent itself to the title of her book, ***Perseverance: How a Determined Athlete Tenaciously Overcame a Stroke***. Marie is truly an inspiration, a wonderful role model, and a cherished friend.

Dedication and Acknowledgements

I have many people that I want to thank for making my dream of writing a book come true. First and foremost, to my incredible family. I want to extend a very loving dedication to my Mom, Rosemary, who has been my patient teacher, my advocate, and cheerleader throughout my life. She has instilled in me a deep faith which has brought me through my toughest times. My Dad, who I know is watching me from Heaven. I carry his spirit with me throughout my life, but especially when I am playing sports. I know he is cheering me on and I'm proud to carry on his legacy. To my siblings, who have grown with me and helped me through not only the process of writing a book, but the process of growing as a person. My boys, David and Michael and their families. Seeing your families grow is a powerful incentive for me. And to John, my partner. You have stood by me through my stroke and without your quick response the day of my stroke, this book probably wouldn't have been possible. Through every part of my recovery from the stroke, you were unwaveringly strong and encouraging. Donna is my inspiration! Without her, I wouldn't have been able to do the book. She is forever cherished! To Chet and Kathleen Doyle, your input and honest feedback has been appreciated throughout this process. Without the positivity of my dear family, boyfriend and friends, I would not have been able to complete this book. Thank you all.

Author's profits from the sale of this book will go to the American Stroke Association.

Transition Piece

My mission in life is to help other people. My passion is pacing. You may be wondering what "pacing" is. In distance running, a pacer's job is to help the people make and achieve their time for each mile. It's not as simple as you may think! For me it's personal. It's about connecting with my "pacees." I meet with my group of runners about 20 minutes before the marathon begins. I introduce myself to my group and in turn, they introduce themselves to me and each other. It never ceases to amaze me what a small world it really is. When the runners tell the group where they are from, it invariably happens that someone else in the group is also from that state. It doesn't matter where the marathon is being held, those connections just keep coming. During the 26.2 mile journey, I help my group of runners physically, emotionally, spiritually, and mentally by running alongside them and pacing them.

I had never run with a pacer before. In fact, I didn't know what a pacer was! That changed on March 7, 2004 in Little Rock, Arkansas at Mile 12 to be exact. I felt alone. I saw a runner carrying a sign that said "4:00." I was intrigued by his sign and his spunk! I ran up next to him to get more information. I asked him a series of questions including "Can anyone run with you? Have you been holding that sign the whole time? Does your arm get tired from holding the sign?." With a beaming smile, he invited me to run next to him and five other runners hoping to finish the race in 4 hours, as his sign indicated.

I crossed the finish line at 3:54:39, almost 5 minutes ahead of the 4 hour pace. I was the only one from the group who finished with him. It was then that I vowed to pace the race the following year, but I had a few "pacing ideas" of my own. The wheels in my head were turning. I pictured myself wearing elaborate hats and balloons as I encouraged my group to run with me. He was a good pacer, but I knew I could take it up a notch!

I had my work cut out for me. I bought a bag of balloons, but I'd have to pace myself! The balloons would have to wait until I officially became a pacer. But for now the bag of balloons represented my goal to help other runners with their experience. I contacted my friend, Mark Bravo, who is the race director in Oklahoma City and the "Chicks in Charge," Gina and Geneva of Little Rock, Arkansas to express my interest in becoming a pace leader. They whole-heartedly encouraged me to pursue my goal.

And this is how my pacing story started……….

1

Back Story

My name is Marie Bartoletti. I have run 428 marathons—109 of them (and counting) since I had a massive stroke in November, 2015. I have aggressively fought back from my stroke and demonstrated consistent perseverance towards my life goals.

I wear many hats including mother……

Physical education teacher…

Girlfriend…

and Athlete.

I have appeared on the cover of the Wheaties Energy Crunch box.

Oh, and I had a massive stroke that nearly ended my passion for running.

My Father at Notre Dame

My Father at North Catholic High School, Pittsburgh, Pennsylvania.

This is my back story. I was the third child (and first girl) born to Rosemary and Richard Soisson in Kalamazoo, Michigan. My parents had four boys and three girls. With four sons and three daughters, my father would lovingly joke that if they had another boy, they would have their own "Soisson" basketball team. Dad didn't realize at the time that girls could play too. Athletics were very important to my Dad. Born in Pittsburgh, he attended North Catholic High School. He pitched for the baseball team, quarterbacked the football team, and played center in basketball

In 1942, two weeks after high school ended, Dad enlisted in the Army Air Corps. Pearl Harbor was bombed on December 7, 1941 and America joined the Allies in WWII. He remained in the

Air Corps until 1946 as a fighter pilot and flew many combat missions over Germany. He also coached basketball in the Air Corps. After the war, Dad received an athletic scholarship for football at Notre Dame. He impressed the coaches and staff so much, that he was the starting quarter back during his freshman year! As sophomore year approached, he was playing softball and sustained a knee injury. Despite extensive efforts to rehab his knee, the injury ended his budding athletic career. Dad liked coaching so much he defied his father's wishes to be an engineer and became a teacher instead. My Dad felt he should share his gifts: coaching and teaching. Dad was very satisfied and proud of how his life turned out.

My Mom, Rosemary, was born in South Bend, Indiana; the third child in the Hein family. When Mom was only three years old, her father was killed while riding to work on his motorcycle and my maternal grandmother became sole parent to three young children. With a strong Catholic faith and fluency in German (language and culture), she made sure that my Mom received piano and voice lessons. Mom had an angelic voice and sang in the church choir. Growing up, Mom was very studious and intelligent and starred in spelling bees. She took a job at a Catholic publisher (Ave Maria Press) in South Bend.

There were seven children in my Dad's family; three boys and four girls. As adults, three of them took religious vows upon entering a convent or seminary. As my Dad reflected on his desire to also enter the priesthood, his own "beautiful angel" entered into his life. Mom and Dad's paths crossed in South Bend. Dad was struck by her beauty, both inside and out. He asked her to a YMCA dance and that is where it all started. My parents were married on March 27, 1951. Dad took his first teaching job at St. Paul Catholic School in Owosso, Michigan. Although my parents loved the town of Owosso, an opportunity was presented to my Dad as head football coach, junior varsity basketball coach and social studies teacher at St. Augustine School in Kalamazoo, Michigan.

The month of March became increasingly important in the Soisson family beginning with my parents' wedding on

March 27th. Three hundred and 63 days later (a day shy of one year), they welcomed their first son, my brother, Richard (Rick). Three years later TO THE DAY, Jim came tumbling out. I must've been aiming for a "best time" even out of the womb, because there were only two years between me and my brother, Jim. Mom and Dad were on a roll with having perfect children. Tom came exactly 13 months after me. From then on, my parents resumed the three-year pattern with John, born in 1961, Kathleen coming in 1964, and my youngest sister, Anne arriving in 1967. Mom must've kept track of the calendar! It would later occur to me that if I would've taken longer to lace up my infant running shoes, each child would've been born exactly three years apart. I was bucking the system from the start.

The year is now 1956, my Dad was teaching and coaching at St. Augustine, which became our family's parish. The family had been living in Kalamazoo for two years when I came

My Parents and siblings as young children, 1970

along. I was the first to be baptized at St. Augustine's (my two older brothers were baptized at St. Paul's back in Owosso, Michigan). Dad was teaching and coaching full time and found that it wasn't enough, so to help increase his skills and income, he began to work on his master's degree at Western Michigan University and to establish a baseball program at St. Augustine Cathedral School. The following year, in addition to taking more post-grad classes and working, he became the athletic director for the school! 1957 was a whirlwind year for my father, and he must've been taking his Geritol to keep his energy up, because I was born in August of 1957! In 1961, Dad received his master's degree from W.M.U. My father was a very humble man, and no fanfare or fuss was made when he got his master's. He chose to stay at home with his family instead.

We practiced the Roman Catholic faith. We attended Mass every Sunday and my Dad, my sister Kathleen, and I served as lectors who read Bible passages to the congregation. When I was born, August 2, 1957, my Dad went to Mass and waved a pink bandana to announce my birth. That pink bandana will be a special symbol later in my life.

Finishing a 100 mile bike ride in Grand Rapids, Michigan with my Dad at the finish line

The annual "May Altar" was a family activity. My brother, Rick, constructed the altar and our neighbors gave us roses to adorn the altar. We then gathered around and prayed as a family. Fish sticks were on the menu on Fridays along with my Mom's homemade macaroni and cheese and tuna noodle casserole.

On Saturdays, Mom made sure we had a special treat—hot dogs, since we weren't allowed to have meat on Fridays. Afterwards, we would all gather to watch Lawrence Welk. My siblings and I attended St. Augustine Catholic School from grades 1-8 and Hackett High School (also the parochial school, where my Dad was the athletic director, coached several sports, and taught Economics and History). I witnessed my parents in outward and quiet ways leading good Catholic lives.

I remember one time I passed my parents' room and saw my Dad kneeling at the side of his bed. He had his head bowed and didn't see me, but I saw him and it meant a lot to me. Before and after each meal, we would offer prayers of thanks as a family. As children, it was instilled in us that we respect our elders, and those in authority; including teachers, police officers, and the neighbors, who were to be addressed as "Mr. and Mrs." The Virgin Mary was, and continues to be, very important to the family. My Mom's favorite color is blue and so is mine. The Virgin Mary is often shown in the color blue as well. To this day, my mom and I say the rosary over the phone together every day.

Christmas with seven kids was always magical and Mom and Dad made sure to preserve the magic for each of us. We went to midnight Mass, which is a long service beginning in a dark church with the congregation lighting candles. I remember Dad getting on us about holding our candles straight up because we four older kids would try to drip candle wax on each other.

After church, we would arrive home to a stack of Kalamazoo Gazette newspapers on the driveway. Rick, Jim, and Tom shared a paper route, but on Christmas, it was a family affair. Anne and Kathleen, the youngest kids, folded the papers. Then we older kids loaded them into sacks and delivered them. The rest of us would finish up and our brother Jim would take a long time. We finally asked him what was taking so long, and he said he stopped to pet the neighborhood cats, dogs, and bunnies. That was cute! Back home, we debated about passing out the gifts, but not in the typical way that brothers and sisters debate about Christmas presents. We wanted to be the one to GIVE the gift and weren't concerned about receiving the presents. The tradition was that we would open one sibling present and that was it. Our parents were outnumbered and they knew it! They had a game plan from the very start. The game plan came in handy, especially on Christmas morning when chaos could have started! On Christmas morning, the first child up would make rounds and wake the others. We stayed in our pj's and took our respective spots on the steps while Dad was getting the camera ready. Dad summoned his inner "Captain Von Trapp" from the Sound of Music. Each child stood patiently on the steps according to age with Anne, the youngest, on the first step. Like I said, they had a game plan! All eyes were then on Anne as we made our way out to the living room. By the time Anne was old enough to fully enjoy the mystique of Christmas, Rick was well on his way to being a young adult. We all went along with Santa's visit so that the youngest children could have the childlike joy of Christmas morning. Seeing the look on Anne and Kathleen's faces brought us our own sense of joy. The youngest child, Anne, was allowed to open her present first and then so on, up the line. The oldest, Rick, waited a long time for his turn, so not only did he receive a gift but he also received the gift of patience! As we gathered around the manger set, we knew it was time to place the Baby Jesus in the cradle. We watched in awe as the train circled the villages, houses, and town square underneath the tree. The lights twinkled on the tree and the train announced its arrival at the railroad crossing with a "choo-choo" and a train whistle.

Birthdays were exceptional at our house and it seemed like there was always a birthday to celebrate. For as long I can remember, my Mom kept a book with each child's name on a page along with their favorite foods for breakfast, lunch and dinner. About a month before our birthday, we checked the book and updated our favorites. Mom didn't even have to remind us to check the book, we remembered it! I can still picture that blue book. I was on page three.

My page read as follows: Breakfast-Cocoa Krispies, Lunch-Tuna Noodle Casserole, and Dinner-Lasagna with lemon cake for dessert. My Mom made an awesome lemon cake; my mouth waters just thinking about it. Mom, with her artistic talent, decorated the cake beautifully with her own homemade icing and my name spelled out in cheese curl snacks. Yes, you read that correctly. Cheetos atop my lemon cake. It was complimented by strawberry ice cream. An iron stomach for a future "Iron Man!" Although the special meals were meant only for the birthday child, I invited my brothers to have Chocolate Rice Krispies, my favorite cereal, since the chocolately coating would make chocolate milk at the bottom of the bowl. Food prices were costly back then, especially for our large family. So, these meals were such a special treat and I looked forward to that special bowl of cereal instead of the usual Wheaties or Cheerios.

We were lucky to have Grandma Hein, my Mom's mother from South Bend. Our other grandparents were deceased, so Grandma Hein was the matriarch of the family. Grandma Hein didn't drive, so my parents would drive her back and forth for family celebrations. There were times when my parents weren't able to drive to get her, so my Grandma would take a bus or train to Kalamazoo to be with us. I remember walking up to her as she got off the bus. Grandma wasn't very tall, and neither was I at that time, and I remember how great it felt to hug her. She was at our house for Christmas, Easter, and birthdays. Grandma Hein was deaf on one side so us kids had to talk a little bit louder so she could participate in dinner conversation. Talking loudly never seemed to be a problem for a family with seven kids!

I was fortunate because my birthday was in the summer. I didn't have to wait for a weekend to have a birthday party. One time, I had four friends over for a Twister party. Everyone was so excited! Not only did Mom prepare dinner for four additional mouths, but she allowed me to have a sleepover party that year. My brothers and I had tents, so it looked like a mini army camp in our backyard that night!

Growing up in a large family was hard at times but the house was always filled with energy and conversation and laughter. My parents encouraged each of us to try new things and be active. After school, we hopped off the bus, changed out of our school uniforms and went out to the yard. Our yard was the best spot in the neighborhood and all of the kids would join us. Dad would still be at work, coaching the teams, and my Mom would be inside preparing a homemade meal and doing laundry for seven children— a LOT of laundry. One summer I took a job as a counselor at "Camp Echo" and my Mom willingly did the laundry for all four counselors! My older brothers trimmed the yard and made a baseball diamond in the backyard in the spring and a football field in the fall with the pine trees acting as the goal line. In the front yard there was a basketball hoop that we played with in the summer. Our favorite basketball game to play was HORSE or PIG depending on how much time we had. We also played four-on-four basketball games. We had mats in the basement where we would blow off steam. The brothers liked to wrestle with each other and depending upon the day, the sisters would be the cheerleaders or join in the horse play. My first word was "ball" and I grew to be quite a tomboy. My nickname is "Fish" because I love the water.

I don't know where Mom found the time to do it all. I was always so proud of my parents and raised my hand to volunteer Mom for chaperoning field trips to the Nature Center, cheerleading camp, and lots of other stuff. Looking back, I probably should have taken her busy schedule into account, but she did it all with a smile. It was always special when Mom packed my lunch and included a little note. One note in particular stands out. When I didn't make the cheerleading squad, my note that day, in Mom's distinctive handwriting said, "Smile, God loves you!" She always knew just what to say and made each of us feel special. Those notes meant so much to me, it was a tradition I carried on with my own sons later in my life. My son, David, also recognized the importance of these notes. When I was substitute teaching, he slipped a note in my lunch bag along with my yogurt. Yes, you never know when someone needs those little notes of encouragement, but my family always has a keen sense of timing for encouraging, each other. My Mom would ring the dinner bell, which meant it was time to come in. I sat next to my Dad at the dinner table and he would slide his mushrooms over to me on Chicken Cacciatore nights. Although he loved the meal, he wasn't a fan of mushrooms, but I was. Even though Dad had put in a long day, he would always tell stories and jokes at the dinner table. My speed came into play there too, cutting ahead of my brothers and sisters to tell my story. The rule was, no TV or phone during dinner, but who needed it when we had so much live entertainment. My parents were sticklers for Clean Plate Club, and sat at the table as long as it took us to clear our plates. "Kids in China are starving!" I became quite skilled at storing peas in my cheeks like a chipmunk would store nuts. Once my plate was clear and my cheeks were full, I would quietly ask to be excused so I could promptly spit them into the toilet. Don't tell Mom!! We had meat, vegetables, fruit, and dessert at each meal. My mom offered us orange juice in the "R" months, (September through March) because we were "not getting enough sunshine" in our lives! If I ever slouched during dinner, Mom poked me in the back to sit up, saying "posture!"

There was a chore chart that was our daily To Do Bible. The "Bible" was really a calendar! On the calendar was washing, drying, and putting the dishes away. Rick would wash the dishes then hand them to Jim to dry. Next, Jim handed me the dishes to put away. Tom was responsible for sweeping. The next week, we would rotate chores. Regardless of the job I had, I would always ask to trade with one of my siblings.

The stereo was playing Big Band music. We sang songs by Mitch Miller, Guy Lombardo, Bing Crosby, Nat King Cole, and Frank Sinatra. My mom, Anne, and Jim were very good singers. They performed in the Notre Dame Glee Club, college bands and piano bars on the Jersey Shore. Later they sang at weddings and in church choirs. My sister, Kathleen, and I both played piano like Mom, but I didn't last long—I hated sitting still for a half hour to practice!

Singing wasn't for me, so I played sports with my brothers. My older brothers, Rick and Jim, were good at golf, while my younger brothers, Tom and John, played football for my dad's team in the fall and tennis in the spring. Kathleen read books 24/7, except when she was doing plays. Anne was a cheer leader and marched in the band. I did every sport I could—golf, softball (a pitcher like my dad), volleyball, basketball, and tennis. The one sport I hated was running. I started playing tennis when I moved to Pittsburgh, where I was in the PTL tennis league and then played in the Mt. Lebanon USTA league. We advanced to the state, and regional levels in Princeton, New Jersey, and national tournament finals in Palm Springs, California where I was #1 singles in the 3.5 levels. (Level 4 meant pro).

Sports and music have continued to be important to my family. All of my siblings' children, and my own, have excelled in the athletic and music departments. My son, David, made tapes for me of my favorite songs when he left for college, knowing I would love to hear his piano playing when he was gone. He played at my mom and dad's 50th anniversary celebration and also at dad's funeral.

Like all families, we had many small traditions. For example, there was a pizza shop in my hometown that we ordered from on Fridays after my dad's football games. We also went there for all seven 8th grade graduations, and even my mom's 85th birthday party. "Bruno's Pizza" is like part of the family!

My Parents and siblings as adults

Parents' 50th Wedding Anniversary, 2001

I met, and became friends with Mark Bartoletti when I coached tennis in Pittsburgh. However, I got a wonderful job offer in Mesa, Arizona and began a new chapter in my teaching career as a business teacher. Thankfully, Dad had encouraged me to major in physical education and minor in business education. I coached volleyball in Mesa and took the team to the state championships where they won. The next few months were a whirlwind. I returned to Pittsburgh over Thanksgiving and Mark proposed to me. We were married December 31, 1982 at my family's house in Kalamazoo. I resigned from my teaching job and returned to Pittsburgh. Although I was sad to leave the staff and students in Mesa, I quickly found a secretarial job back home. Then I got a job at Sacred Heart teaching physical education in grades 1-12. I Loved it!

As a young adult, I was a representative for Christmas Around the World/House of Lloyd, where I won a trip to Acapulco for being first place in sales. I won top salesperson and was awarded many trips including to Hawaii, and Egypt.

When I was a teenager, I went to the beach with my good friend and I remember her pointing to my feet and asking, "What is wrong with your feet?" while pointing to my bunions. I was horrified and as I aged, the bunions became larger until they were no longer bearable. My doctor was hesitant to perform the surgery because he feared they would grow back. It was no longer an option, I HAD to have the surgery in 1991. At night, the pain became excruciating. My doctor told me to forego running and opt to swim and bike. So, what did I do? I completed an IRONMAN triathlon (shhh, don't tell the podiatrist)! Surgery was considered to be successful. Unfortunately, my godfather, Mr. Rapacz, passed away that same week. Mr. Rapacz was a tall man, and an assistant coach for my father. He was also an NFL player for Oklahoma and a skilled artist. My heart was heavy when he passed, not only because I would miss him dearly, but also because of my recent surgery I wouldn't be able to travel for his funeral.

Mark and I were planning a trip to Stone Mountain in Vermont with the boys. We were looking forward to skiing over Easter weekend. We made arrangements to stay with our friend, Margaret

Ferguson, who had a beautiful home nestled amongst the gorgeous scenery. It was an awesome weekend and some delicious Ben and Jerry's ice cream to boot!

We enjoyed traveling with the boys who were always well-behaved. Our next journey took us to Arizona to see as much as we could. On our list were the Grand Canyon, Zion National Park, Yellowstone and a few other places. But, when I found out you could buy an Eagle pass, and save money if you end up visiting six or seven National parks, it became my goal to visit as many as possible in the next week and a half. This was to the initial excitement and later annoyance of my sons. At our visit to the Grand Canyon, the rangers were warning people not to try to make it to the river and back in one day, but I did it anyway. I had forgotten about that, but apparently it stuck with my son, David, as a 14 year-old boy. He reminded me of it recently. It wasn't the first or last time my family would be worried about me because of a physical undertaking. To make the most of our Eagle Pass we then traveled around to visit Bryce Canyon, Zion, Petrified Forest, Yosemite, Death Valley,

Christmas around the World first place sales—a trip to Acapulco

Trip to Acapulco with my parents

Redwood Forest, and also spent time in Lake Powell and Hoover Dam, and Montezuma's Castle. At Yosemite, I was fortunate to hike and scale the famous Half-Dome Trail, which was 15 miles in length. This took about seven hours and rose to 4,800 feet, with an exhilarating final 400 feet that required an ascent using cables attached to the rock.

We spent one or two nights in Las Vegas in the Circus Circus hotel and had a fantastic time. There was an indoor roller coaster. We then drove to a Dude ranch with conestoga wagons. Michael and David got to try skeet shooting, which they really enjoyed. We stayed a night, and the next morning took a helicopter into the Grand Canyon to raft down the Colorado River. We camped along the riverbank for a few nights. I don't fear race mileage, but I do fear snakes, and I saw plenty in the river.

We ended the trip staying with friends in San Diego. After our National Park extravaganza, I think everyone was relieved to relax a bit by the beach (and the TV) for a few days.

Yosemite National Park

In 2003, I was very honored to be considered for the cover of the Wheaties Energy Crunch box. There were 5000 entrants. I was notified that I was going to have my NAME appear on the box and I was invited to New York City for the unveiling of the cover. The five finalists took the stage and as the box was uncovered by famed gymnast, Mary Lou Retton, I saw my picture on the front. For a moment, I thought each of the finalists were being shown a prototype of what their cover might look like if they won. And then it hit me, I HAD WON!!! I was awarded $10,000 which I donated to the American Heart Association.

Meeting Mary Lou Retton at the unveiling of the Wheaties box.

With renewed ambition, fresh off the Wheaties accomplishment, I set a new goal to complete a marathon in every state. I completed the feat in 2004-2005. My 50th (titanium) marathon was in Honolulu, Hawaii on December 11, 2005. Mission accomplished!

Pennies became an important symbol

I used to call my Dad at least three times a week, even just to say hi. Five days after my father died in 2009, I made a 100 mile run. It was my birthday, and I wore a pink shirt to commemorate my dad waving the pink handkerchief the day I was born. I won the race, took my shirt off and waved it in the air, thinking of him, and knowing he was with me! On the day of my dad's funeral, I ran to St. Augustine, the church where we were all baptized and now the place he would have his "last mass." When I got there, the priest gave me a host and a hug. I was crying. I kept running, toward the football field named after him. A police officer let me in so I could run across the field and back. I wanted to be on his field, because I was never able to cheer (officially) for his teams when I was in high school. Along the way, I picked up some pennies. When I got home, it struck me that I had collected seven pennies—one for each of my brothers and sisters and me! I started looking at the dates on them and realized that each one correlated to a birth year or another important event in our lives. I didn't know how I could go on without him.

A month before Dad passed away, I was visiting my parents. My room was next to their room. At about 2:30 a.m. I heard someone calling my name. I thought, "That can't be my Dad calling for me" because he was on a ventilator and his voice was weak. I went to their room and found my Mom fast asleep and Dad calling me over to talk. I sat on the edge of his bed. I couldn't believe my eyes. He didn't appear or sound like he was sick. True to form, Dad was continuing to teach me. As we talked he said, "Your mother is like a queen. Treat her like that. I want you kids to stick together and avoid battles." I agreed and gave him a kiss goodnight. I didn't sleep the rest of the night because I was shocked at how well Dad looked and the urgency of his message. That turned out to be our last conversation. He delivered a similar message to

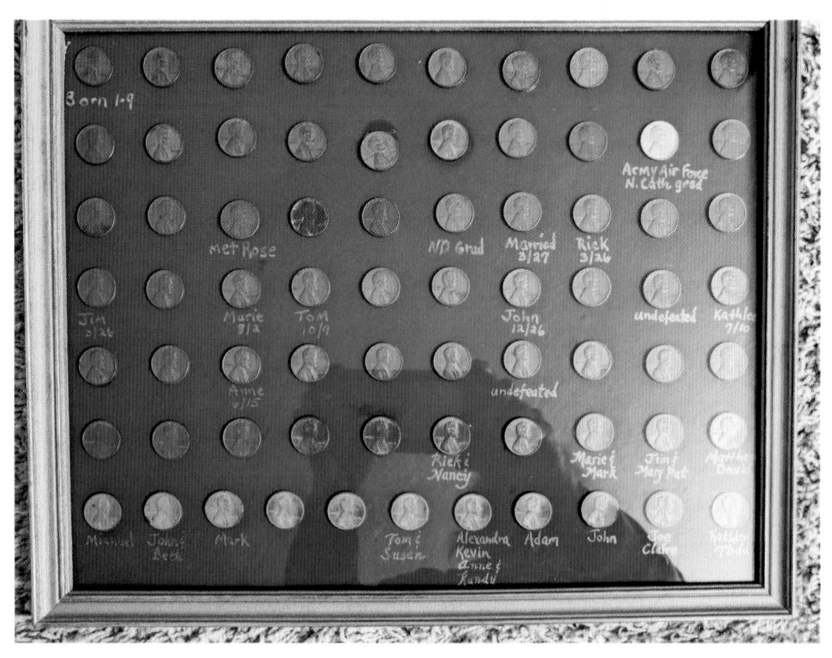

Dad's 70th Birthday Pennies

my sister, Anne. Hospice was tending to him, but Dad was still trying to tend to us kids.

I received Dad's football coaching jacket and upon wearing it, I felt immediately closer to him. I still wear his jacket and it continues to bring me strength and courage. Can you see the resemblance?

Me, posing as My Father | My Father, Coach Soisson

Dad's passing took a toll on my mom. She was in a daze for months. Unfortunately, I had to return to Pittsburgh. I missed the routine and connection of calling my Dad throughout the week. My mom missed her husband so much, I made sure to continue to call her for our daily recitation of the Rosary, a tradition we have kept to this day.

As time went on, we all started a "new normal," back to our work, children, and day-to-day activities. Mom picked up the pieces and tried to live normally the best she could after losing the love of her life. New traditions began. My brother Tom's house and my sister Anne's house became the gathering places for Easters and Thanksgivings. Tom's house is three miles from Notre Dame. My nephew is in the Glee Club at Notre Dame so we went to hear him sing at Easter Mass on campus.

In retrospect, I now realize that losing my Dad had made me turn up the pace on my own athletic pursuits. I dedicated my time to running, cycling, swimming, and playing tennis. These sports grew into a passion for me, just as my Dad had a passion for coaching, basketball, football and anything sports related. He had definitely passed this along to me and I was bound and determined to continue in his footsteps.

I joined three running groups: Steel City Road Runners, where I was a pacer, People Who Run Downtown, and Chickentown Road Runner Club in Somerset, PA where my boyfriend, John, lives. I met John through a mutual friend, Paul, at a baseball game in 2010. John and I ran with the Chickentown group who quickly became good friends of ours. It was enjoyable to run in a rural area with this group. John lived on a farm in this area. Our discussions often included talk about whose goat was producing milk and whose chickens were laying the most eggs. John was quite proud of his goats and prolific chickens. I met Kathy and Ward Shumaker from the Chickentown group and we hit if off right away. When John and I headed to Richmond, Virginia for a marathon, it was Kathy and her husband, Ward, who stepped up and tended to John's precious goats.

I enjoyed running with the "People Who Run Downtown." My best friends, David Timko, Heather Riese, Jim Karn, Tony Defeo, and Joann Avrand, and I ran four to six miles every Tuesday or Thursday. We'd choose a meeting spot, typically a bar or restaurant and a start time, usually 6:00 p.m. Pittsburgh is a "defined" city—defined by its tunnels and bridges—and Pittsburghers are very proud of it. Several areas come together at the confluence of the Allegheny and Monongahela Rivers to form the Ohio River. It is an amazing sight to behold. Once you make it through the "tunnel traffic" near the mouth of the Fort

Pitt Tunnel, the end of the tunnel leads to many visitors' first beautiful view of the city and Point State Park with its immense fountain. People, including myself, are in awe of the spectacular entrance to Downtown Pittsburgh.

After working all day as a physical education teacher and coaching tennis at Thomas Jefferson High School, I would swiftly speed Downtown to meet up with "People Who Run Downtown." Most of the time even my GPS wasn't sure where I was going. Once I'd get to the bar or restaurant to meet the other members of the running group, parking was the next distressing thing to overcome. Running wasn't the hard part of being a member of this group. Driving and parking Downtown were the real challenges. I wasn't a fan of paying to park and parking was free after 6 p.m. Here's where the story turns into an elementary school math problem: "If a determined runner drives around Downtown Pittsburgh for seven minutes looking for a free place to park after 6 pm, how many watermelons will she need before the train leaves the station?" That sums up the parking situation in town. I wasn't happy when I was driving in traffic or trying to park my car, but I was eager to see the other members of the group and pumped when I actually got there and started to run with them. We ran for an hour (six miles) and we chatted along the way. It was an opportunity to meet a lot of new people and forge new friendships.

On my way home, I visited Healthtrax for the second time each day. I was at Healthtrax from 5:30-6:30 a.m. to swim while reciting the Rosary. My evening visit consisted of cycling and lifting. Once I returned home at 9 p.m., I would eat and go to bed. Except one day out of each month, I'd come home and bake something delicious for our school's faculty meeting.

A special event for our group was the annual "Christmas Lights" run. Thursday night, two weeks before Christmas, our group met for the run. Bob, the Fleet Feet manager, and Deb, the assistant manager, set up a booth in the PPG Wintergarden raising money for charity, surrounded by all of the gingerbread houses. The spirit of Christmas was in the air and the crisp

Fleet Feet Crew—Bob, Marie, and Deb

winter air pinched our faces as we ran. It was like Christmas all over again in Kalamazoo. It is exquisite! When we ran past the Nativity scene in the city, our group would stop to pray and then continue to run.

I was blessed to initiate the Kids of Steel program in Pittsburgh. The goal of the organization is to engage young runners to train four months to build up from one mile to 25 miles. Their 26th mile was accomplished on the Saturday before the Pittsburgh Marathon at the "Kids Marathon." When the program started, I had 76 student participants at my school and 300 students sign up in Pittsburgh. In 2017, the number of participants grew to an astounding 8,000 students. I am proud to see the program continue to grow and foster a love of running in young people. My marathon buddies are beginning similar programs in other states as well.

I had the pleasure of coaching both boys and girls tennis from 2010-15 at Thomas Jefferson High School under the direction of Chuck Correll. The students were a lively bunch, full of energy and eager to learn all of the nuances of the game.

Thomas Jefferson Boys Tennis Team

Thomas Jefferson Girls Tennis Team

Chiro Joe and Me

Chuck was so helpful and took a genuine interest in developing my coaching skills. I was blessed to have him as a tennis coach/mentor. Chuck was a healthy man, until he had a stroke in his 50s. After I had my stroke in 2015, Chuck would graciously take me to my appointments and talk to me in the car. His words resonated with me and I was so appreciative to spend time with a fellow athlete and stroke survivor. He understood what I was going through.

Around this time, I also sustained a lower back injury. I tried to work and run through the pain, but realized I needed professional help. One of my fellow teachers had told me about Dr. Joe Mele, a chiropractor whose office was only a mile away from my school building. I stopped in and found him to be fabulous. Not only did he tend to my back, but also addressed my sciatica. His approach instilled confidence in me and I continue to seek his services whenever needed. He is a valuable member of my "team."

Since not every marathon is in my hometown, my itinerary includes a lot of traveling. In my opinion, flying is the worst part of a marathon. There are a lot of flights to book, weather delays, and finding a place to stay close to the race. I travel almost every weekend and after all of that stress, I often need to breathe and relax.

Birth/raising kids-November 1984

I was riding a stationary bicycle and doing a needlepoint project while in my third trimester of my first pregnancy. I awoke with stomach pain during my 8th month thinking that I had indigestion from the dinner the night before. My volleyball team had graciously given me a gift certificate for a buffet-style restaurant. I did lot of eating that night! So naturally, I thought when I had stomach pain that it was just from the extensive meal. Because it was my first pregnancy, I didn't even realize that my water had begun to break. My then husband, Mark, placed a call to my obstetrician at 3:00 a.m. The doctor told to wait a while because it may be "false labor." By 5:00 a.m., the pain was excruciating and the doctor told us to head to Magee

Hospital in downtown Pittsburgh. By 9:00 a.m., I was delivering a baby! The obstetrician told me that if I had not been in such tip-top shape, my labor and delivery would be harder than it was. The doctor said he was better than the Pittsburgh Pirate's catcher when he "caught" David being born. David was quick, but the doctor's reaction "at the plate" was even faster. My precious baby, David, had arrived in the world a month early and needed to stay in intensive care for a week. I felt nervous and helpless. Mark helped me a lot through those times and feelings. A week later I was able to bring David home! David started his life at 5lbs, 5oz and 19inches but he steadily grew up to be a tall, muscular man.

Although motherhood was new to me, I quickly assumed the role and loved it. Thirteen months later, my angel-baby Michael came into this world. One look at him and I was instantly in love. He spent a period of time in intensive care also. Having two babies so close together presented some challenges. I had to strategically plan my day, even down to bathroom trips. I would pack up the boys and go on outings to the library, friends' houses and grocery store trips. I loved showing off my beautiful boys. They were always so well behaved. Their manners were fantastic. Waitresses would comment how wonderful their manners were. "Please" and "Thank you" were taught early on in our house. Mark's parents would host Sunday dinner every week. We spent Thanksgiving and Easter with my side of the family in Kalamazoo, Michigan. The boys adapted well to the 400 mile car ride.

Along with the Tupperware craze, Christmas Around the World was becoming popular. I saw an ad for it in the Pennysaver and decided to give it a try. Mark didn't want me going back to work, but I thought this would be a way to make extra money while staying home with the kids. I enjoyed the social aspect. Mark stayed home with the kids, and I got to go to parties every night! I earned family trips to Hawaii, Egypt, and many other places as a reward for my sales. In Egypt, my sister, Anne, and David went horseback riding on WILD horses.

Marie, Mark, Michael, David, 2001

David was so scared (poor thing!) but it prepared him for the next day's camel riding through Cairo. We got our picture taken on the camels and ended up with a Christmas card that looked just like the Nativity.

I sold tree toppers, ornaments, centerpieces, and other Christmas decorations for almost a decade. I usually was ready for a break by the time Christmas came around, and made Mark and the kids put up all of our Christmas decorations without me.

When I switched jobs to work for another home decorating company, my schedule changed. I only worked from June through December, but still managed to be the number One demonstrator and supervisor, with 23 demonstrators working under me. I scheduled a demonstration every night. My perseverance was evident. I finally was able to put in the swimming pool that I always wanted in our backyard. The boys loved it as much as I did.

As the years passed, David and Michael continued to grow up. Pretty soon, David was off to University of Dayton in 2003, and Michael went off to Kent State in 2004. While it was a joy

My Sons, 2008

David and me on his wedding day, 2012

Michael on his wedding day with his brother David, 2011

to see my kids all grown, it was sad to see them go. David made me a tape of his music which I listened to every day. This made the transition a little bit easier. Around the time that the boys went to college, Mark and I decided to divorce. I too, was ready to start a new chapter.

Stroke -2015

In November, I returned home with my boyfriend, John, to Kalamazoo, Michigan to celebrate Thanksgiving with my family. Thursday morning at 7:42 a.m. I was going into my room and John said, "Are you OK?" That was the last thing I remember. I was unaware anything was going on. "You are having a stroke! Lay down on the floor." John continued speaking, but I could not hear him. John is a fireman, he knew the symptoms and called the ambulance. I was rushed to the Bronson emergency room. Several attempts were made to contact my sons, David and Michael, for consent to administer TPA (a clot-breaking drug). These were not successful. John could not give authorization to allow TPA consent (legal BS). The next in line for consent is a sibling. I have six brothers and sisters. John called my brother, Tom, who is a pediatrician in South Bend, Indiana. After the doctor explained the risk/reward to Tom, he gave consent.

The TPA was administered, and after several minutes John said to the doctor, "This is not working, is it?." The doctor replied, "Not the way we would like." So I was prepped for the cath-lab. The catheterization was somewhat successful and the clot broke up when the doctor attempted to remove it. Late Thursday morning, after returning from the cath-lab, I remember I was lying in a hospital bed. I was told I had a stroke (score 25). According to the National Institute of Health, a stroke score of 25 was in the "severe" range. I had an ischemic stroke that blocked my left medial cerebral artery.

I saw John and my brother, Tom, from South Bend, and my sister, Anne, from Cleveland. I couldn't speak! I understood everything that was being said to me. I spent the rest of the afternoon hooked to several monitors and resting, as more family members came to visit. John spent the night which was pretty uneventful. On Friday, the seriousness of my situation was starting to sink in when my son, David, arrived from Maine. The nursing staff was constantly monitoring my condition. Physical Therapy and Occupational Therapy staff were there. The physical therapist was checking my left to right strength deficit, when she discovered that I was quite strong. She said, "Grab my hand and pull", and I almost pulled her over. When they told me I could walk, I jumped out of bed. Everyone stopped me because I was still connected to all of my monitors. Ben, the registered nurse who walked with me, was quite impressed with how far and fast I walked. He said I had to turn around and go back because he had other patients.

The occupational therapist took me to the occupational therapy room where they tested my ability to turn a key and doorknob, climb stairs and basic daily activities. I passed with flying colors. They determined that I did not need any physical therapy. It was discovered that I have a PFO, (a hole in my heart). My heart went into A-fib. This caused a clot to form and it passed through my PFO and went to my brain causing my stroke.

Lack of speech hit me the hardest. I couldn't say my name or even answer "yes" or "no". I had to rely on gestures and shaking my head to communicate. I worked on things that had to deal with my swallowing since I had some right side weakness, verbally answering questions, and also imitating oral movements. They say I made progress in the hospital, but I found it hard to believe. I participated in speech therapy until my discharge and it was recommended that I continue services two times per week. I changed it to four times per week.

My cousin, Kathy, a retired nurse, asked me to live with her in Portage, Michigan. She saw this as a win/win situation. She had just lost her husband in July. I was very close to her husband, Sam. I went to his funeral five months before. So she could make me better and I could help her!

I was discharged on Tuesday, ran six miles on Wednesday and every day after that. I got a halter monitor for 30 days that

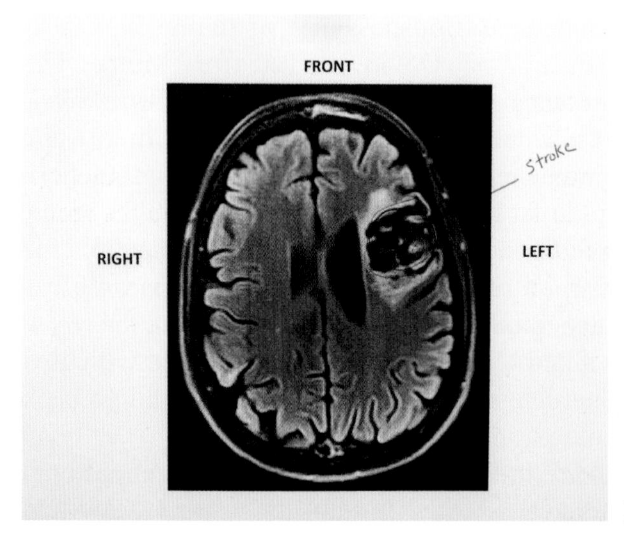

Brain scan.

was on me 24/7. Once while running at Kathy D's with the Holter monitor, I returned home to receive a call from the company monitoring me wirelessly. There was a problem; my blood pressure was low. They were worried. This was me just having fun. From that day forward we would notify them when I was having fun—running!

While living with Kathy, I saw a speech therapist named Heather. Heather was hard! I cried often. She was excellent but I was beginning to realize that something was very wrong with me. I could not understand why I was still unable to speak. I was really having a hard time naming the pictures she showed me and completing every other task she gave me. I was not used to being unable to do something I thought was so easy. We worked very hard and I made some progress, but still needed more therapy. It was Christmastime, and Kathy was playing some Christmas music on the computer. Kathy knew of a famous country singer who stutters, Mel Tellis, but when he sings, he does not stutter. She decided to try that with me so we sang Christmas carols like "Hark the Herald Angels Sing" and it worked! I was able to verbalize and sing along with the songs with no problem. It was my Christmas miracle!

It was a blessing to have two Kathys in my life. A Kathy with a "K" and a Cathy with a "C." Cathy with a "C" was my favorite friend growing up. She came to Bronson Hospital and gave me a Willow Tree Angel. She came over to my cousin, Kathy's, house every day, a 20-minute drive each way. She took me to Costco. We enjoyed trying the free samples and had a few laughs along the way. Laughing felt good.

While recovering in Michigan, I was awash with "get well wishes" from faculty, friends, and family. John's parents sent a very sweet photo. Although all the prayers and messages made me feel loved, my speech precluded me from reciprocating.

After four weeks, I returned to Pennsylvania. I started to live with my good friends, Carol and Tim Lee and their dog, Lucy.

Kathy Dickason and me

Lucy would lick the tears from my cheeks. Carol would know that I was upset by the dog's actions. They introduced me to Buffalo Wild Wings, even though I don't eat meat! I was very happy they were there during some of my VERY difficult times. They started taking me to speech therapy and my doctor's appointments. Speaking of wonderful friends, I want to tell you about my fellow tennis coach, Chuck who also suffered a stroke. Chuck volunteered to take me to my additional speech sessions in the evenings since I was not cleared to drive myself. I didn't like the feeling of being dependent on others, but I realized what wonderful friends I had.

I started outpatient speech therapy with Jackie at Jefferson Hospital in January. Carol brought me for my evaluation and then for therapy sessions since I still was unable to drive. Four days a week with Jackie we worked on picture naming, sound and word pronunciation, sentence formulation, word finding, and intonation. In preparation for returning back to teaching,

Sandra and John Rosatti, Sr.

Carol and Tim Lee with Lucy

we worked on making lesson plans and linking pictures with directions for activities. I also went to Charleroi to see Cindy, a close friend and speech therapist. Cindy worked with me on the days I was not at Jefferson Hospital. I thought that was going to make me better faster. I reduced to three days at Jefferson at the end of February and finished up with Cindy at that time as well. This was not good enough for me, so I had another evaluation done and started therapy at Crossroads Speech and Hearing with Donna and Whitney two days a week. I was back up to five days with one day being a two-a-day. John clocked his therapy time with me every weekend as well. I ate, slept, and breathed speech therapy.

In January, my cardiologist and neurologist said I could run a full marathon, 26.2 miles. I had an opportunity to pace, and it would be therapeutic. Pacing others to complete marathons, whether it's their first or 20th, makes me feel valuable. I needed to feel that again. I began to bike 100 miles a week, lifting and swimming along with running. I ran the Miami marathon on January 24, 2016 with my good friend, Marcela, and we finished in 5 hours and 30 minutes. I didn't know if I could do it. I did it and actually felt like I could have run it faster.

After I got one marathon under my belt, I continued with pacing a marathon just about every week thereafter. When I ran in Little Rock, Arkansas on March 6, I was interviewed for the local news station. When I pace, I always have hats that I wear and a sign that I carry. At the finish line, I was informed I was on TV so I said, "I love to pace." That's all I could say and John filled in with the rest of the interview for me. The reporter remarked, " If you weren't in as good of shape, you wouldn't be here" referring to my athleticism prior to having my stroke. That echoed what my OB/GYN said when I delivered my first child.

It was such a treat to run the Pittsburgh marathon again in May. I also qualified for the Boston Marathon when I ran in my home town of Kalamazoo, Michigan at 4:04 over Mother's Day with John as my pacer. It was nice to be home again and spend time with my Mom, Kathy D. and Cathy R. I sent a video message to my first speech therapist, Heather to keep her updated on my progress. She was so happy to hear from me that she was crying. In September, I met up with Marcela to run again but this time in Berlin, Germany. That was amazing. Other incredible places to pace were Chicago, Niagara Falls and New York City. Running is a blessing and a release that helps me feel like myself again.

It was several months before I was allowed to drive. Getting the okay from my neurologist and passing an eye test was hard for me. Then I was able to move back home and live by myself. That was very hard but the start of things returning to normal, or as close as they could be. In June, I taught P.E. at a Vacation Bible School. Hard, but fun! Thank God for my support system; Mom, Rose, and my sons, David and Michael. Thirteen months after my stroke, I began to say the Rosary with Mom every day. This was done over the phone due to the 400 miles between us. This strong background of faith that Mom instilled in me has helped me get through these tough times.

Then in January, Michael gave me my first grandchild, Hannah. Michael, Ashley and Hannah were a great help with my depression. Then in March, I received another blessing. My son, David, and wife Erin gave me my second granddaughter, Maddie (Maddelina). The birth of my granddaughters was such a blessing and made me want to live.

My sister, Anne, wanted to talk once a week but I had no desire to talk with anyone. I was just not comfortable with my speech. I am still struggling but getting better with it.

Mom and me

Some of the hardest things to overcome were depression, missing my students, and coaching tennis. It is still difficult today. John, Jackie, and Donna say that I am really improving and I am very hard on myself. They are pretty impressive and I love them.

In August, I was denied medical clearance to return to teaching. I was devastated. So, I set out to become a lifeguard at Healthtrax, my local gym and pool, at the USC Recreation Club. I had to take a class for a week and pass a grueling swimming test. I passed with ease! I was set to begin lifeguarding two shifts a day, one at Healthtrax in the morning and one at Upper Saint Clair in the afternoon/evening. This went on for four weeks and I LOVED it! I met many people and formed great relationships. At this point, I had to withdraw from lifeguarding because I found out I was not allowed to accept a paycheck due to being on sick leave from teaching. It was another crushing blow.

Then I went to a psychologist for help. I was fortunate enough that I still had the Stroke Association group that I was attending once a week, and some volunteer work once a week. I loved that. I was visiting my Aunt Lois (Sister Miriam Richard), a retired teacher and therapist at Seton Hill in Greensburg. I'd go there with John and she'd help me with different therapy tasks. One day, we began talking about more volunteer opportunities. I already was volunteering at the library, and my aunt suggested I get in touch with Sister Joyce at Germaine Harbor, an apartment community for seniors. She was my principal at Sacred Heart in Oakland 33 years ago; my first teaching job in Pittsburgh. I contacted her right away and began volunteering there every Wednesday. They liked me so much, they let me attend events such as Bingo and Light Up Night, where I took some homemade Christmas cookies. They loved them.

A walking group was launched with Sister Joyce and the residents of Germaine Harbor

John was instrumental to my recovery. He knew I was lucky to be alive. He did speech therapy every time he was around. I was making my own flight reservations and I told them I had a stroke and they were very patient and supportive. John told me I could do that. He told me I could pace the marathons, and I told the runners I had a stroke. That was a great motivator for them to run with a stroke survivor.

Two of my oldest friends, Cathy Roberts Reed and Sue Anderson, my neighbor across the street in Kalamazoo and I were like the Three Musketeers, Cathy is a year older than me, and Sue a year younger. To this day, we are still close. I am still friends with my grade school and high school friends, although I don't get to see them as much as I would like to. I have made friendships with people all over the United States and throughout the world because of my marathons. Friendships have also been formed from my years of teaching, lifeguarding at the local recreation center and gym, and through volunteer work. Each of these people I care about deeply and they hold a special place in my heart.

I was thankful to spend Groundhog's Day with my Mom in Kalamazoo. She especially likes to play Scrabble and was eager to pose with her winning game board when we played.

Mom and me playing Scrabble

Speaking of being thankful, I returned to Kalamazoo to spend Thanksgiving with my family. I felt uneasy and nervous about going back. The last time I spent Thanksgiving there, I had a stroke. I tried to push that thought out of my mind, but couldn't. But eating Thanksgiving dinner at my brother, John's, house provided a change of scenery that helped me to get through and enjoy the moments. We got a picture of FOUR generations! How blessed!.

David's Family with my Mom and me—4 generations

Ashley, Michael and Hannah Bartoletti

What better way to spend the Christmas holidays than at the beach, with family (Ashley, Hannah, and Michael), AND getting a run in!

This is probably the only time you will see a picture of me and Hannah not moving! She inherited her speed and energy from me, I think.

I've been hearing this for over 15 years that I should write a book. I kept the book as a "back burner" idea until I had my stroke. I am typically a very private person. I tend to keep things to myself, though when I am running a marathon or pacing a marathon, I am the bubbliest person around.

Every runner that I have ever paced has helped me as much, and possibly even more than I have helped them. So now you can see the meaning behind the title of my autobiography, *Perseverance.*

The next part of this book highlights some of my favorite marathons, 100-milers, and Ironman stories.

Hannah and me

Hannah Bartoletti
My how she has grown
and still on the move!

2

Marie's Timeline

1995

5/07/1995 Pittsburgh Marathon, Pennsylvania

My first marathon! This is the one that started it all. I finished at 4:01:48. I learned a lot, some of it the hard way! Three weeks prior in chilly Pittsburgh, I ran 20 miles without hydrating. I thought that was the way to do it. Who wanted to drink something cold on an already chilly day? It seemed to work. The day of the race, I felt nervous and a bit scared. My body felt ready, though. The weather was warmer than during my training. I completed the first half of the marathon in 1:50. I was on pace to complete the marathon in 3:50–not bad for a first timer! Every few miles, volunteers offered water and Gatorade but I didn't want to slow down–not even for a drink. Twenty miles in, my legs fell apart and I realized that I made a critical mistake. I should have had something to drink! At 22 miles, a spectator yelled out, "Come on, you only have 4 miles left!" and I said, "Come on then, you can do it with me!." He declined! I had to do the rest myself. I crossed the finish line and the volunteer told me that I looked dehydrated. Thinking that I knew better than they did, I bypassed the medical tent and opted to go home. On the way home, I had to stop at a gas station to throw up, but I felt a little bit better after that. I made the decision that I was NEVER going to run a marathon again. First time and LAST time! Once home, I took a shower and then settled in to a 20 minute bath. Baths weren't "my thing," but it felt so good to soothe my muscles in the tub. I knew that I needed to go to my substitute teaching job at Ringgold High School the next morning.

5/08/1995 The day started as usual I felt pretty good. I got to work, and the principal made a special announcement, "Marie Bartoletti ran the Pittsburgh Marathon in 4:01." Throughout the day, numerous teachers congratulated me, but one teacher said something to me that resonated. He said, "Geez, I don't even like to drive a car for four hours and you RAN for four straight hours!?" I started to think, "Hmmmm, maybe I can do it again ... just one more time ... and finish in 3:59... oh, and maybe I should hydrate along the way!!"

2000

6/10/2000 Sunburst Marathon, South Bend, Indiana

I stayed at my brother, Tom's, house for 3 days. I had a fabulous time and enjoyed spending time with my nephew and nieces. My parents were there too. I finished in 3:59:48, beating my first marathon time by 2 minutes! The finish line was at Notre Dame Stadium. That was cool.

2001

In 2000 and 2001 my focus was on tennis, competing in district and national tournaments. There were challenges. I found out how expensive it was for court time, equipment and travel. It was also a challenge to find others to play. Men typically did not want to play with me. I never synched up with female players because those at my level were too far away to play regularly. I decided to stop playing tennis competitively even though I had a deep love for the sport. I found running better suited my lifestyle. I could open my front door, start running and not pay a dime! I could run when and where I wanted. Coaching young tennis players could continue my involvement with tennis.

2002

3/03/2002 B&A Trail Marathon, Severna Park, Maryland

Two weeks before the event, my sister, Anne, was visiting from Washington, DC. We went for a 6 mile run together and talked back and forth all the while. Anne said she was interested in running a half marathon with me. Yippee! As luck would have it, the B&A Trail Marathon was basically in her back yard. It was a date.

Anne had given birth to her second child, her first girl, just about two years prior to this race. I felt so proud of her, and excited to be part of her first marathon experience. Anne was going along the race route with a group of three participants and keeping a very good pace time. However, around mile 10, they took off and Anne was not able to keep up with the group's pace and she felt rather alone as the group proceeded on. She needed some encouragement to complete her mission. We Soisson girls don't give up easily! That's when she pulled out her cell phone and placed a call to her husband, Randy. Yes, she placed a phone call in the midst of the race. Randy told her to think of their daughter and focus on the joy of Olivia being born but Anne could only seem to think of the pain associated with childbirth AND the pain she was having with the half marathon. So, out came the cell phone and she called our mom! True to form, Mom was gentle and compassionate with Anne. Just what she needed. Moms always seem to know just what to say. Anne completed her half marathon and then biked the second half with me as I continued to run. I liked it. I liked hearing the sound of her voice and listening to her retell the story of her "Half Marathon Phone Calls" to Mom and Randy. I finished with a time of 3:57:51. Afterwards, Anne put her bike on the back of her car and we drove to her house.

12/07/2002 Reggae Marathon, Bahamas

I met Susie Albert, a coach with Train to End Stroke, at the Upper St. Clair library, in the southern suburbs of Pittsburgh several weeks before the marathon. Train to End Stroke is an organization that takes walkers and runners who have never run a marathon before and shapes them into marathon training. I had coached volleyball and track in years past and wanted to know more about becoming a coach for Train to End Stroke. I was feeling depressed over the passing of Rick Egeland who was a tennis coach at my Thomas Jefferson High School. He was a young, athletic man who sustained a stroke while on the golf course. I had heard of Train to End Stroke and admired the work they did, but during this chance encounter with Susie, it took on a different meaning for me. It was so heartfelt. Susie and I bonded and I was re-energized by her enthusiasm for her organization. Susie helped me take the feelings of sadness over the loss of Rick and channel it into a good thing. I decided immediately that I wanted to dedicate the Reggae Marathon to Rick. Every weekend, Susie and I, and our group of trainees would meet at various parks in Pittsburgh to run together. I had the pleasure of running with a man named Dave, who was a physical therapist. On the day of the Reggae Marathon, I put Rick's name on a bracelet, which I wore for the race, and afterwards gave to his wife, Bonnie. I took first place with 3:52:51, even though I broke my finger 5 steps into the race! In my defense, it was dark at 5 a.m. and I was unable to see the reflector on the road. Reflectors don't serve much purpose when there is no sunlight to reflect! !! Volunteers provided drinks along the race route, and I had to open mine with my teeth since it became evident that I broke my "opposable" thumb during my fall! Ever graceful, I realized that the red sports drink had become a geyser and spouted sticky red juice all over my "good" hand. Not to mention, by that time, the temperature had soared to 90 degrees. I passed several farms and took note of the barnyard animals. The heat and pain from my thumb began to take its toll because I would swear that the cows began to gather at the fence and watch me run—so I "mooed" at them as I passed. My time qualified me for the Boston Marathon. I ran 7 minutes faster than the qualifying time, 4 hours. Dave, from TTES-Pittsburgh, said to me, "You qualified," and I replied, "I did not." I didn't even realize that I needed 4 hours.

Susie and I went snorkeling, kayaking, horseback riding, and played tennis. I met a guy, we played doubles, and won the championship. Rick's Café was the spot where we were listening to music while watching people cliff jump. I decided to join in and my pals said, "You can do it," and I did. I was jumping and held my nose, which made my ear pop. After a flight back home, I went directly to the hospital for my ear and broken thumb. It sure made the doctors laugh!

2003

4/21/2003 My first Boston Marathon

It was such an emotional experience for me that I cried at the starting line during The Star Spangled Banner. I was here! I finished in 3:41:18. I thought I had enough time to do two marathons. If I didn't have to be at work the next day, I would have. I had to hurry to my train to make my flight home without even showering.

Summer 2003. Leesburg, Virginia

I had an idea. I would head towards Washington, DC…on my bike. We are fortunate to live near the Montour Trail, an old railroad track that has been converted into a walking/biking trail. At the time, the trail was not complete, so I had to bike a little off-course to get there. I had to pack light, putting my belongings in a duffle bag strapped to my bike. I found a bed and breakfast along the way and the owners recognized me from my Wheaties box. They took a picture of me with my box and graciously let me stay with them. The trip took 300 miles over the course of two days! My sister, Anne, picked me up in D.C. and when she drove me home, we enjoyed some fun sister time.

11/23/2003 Philadelphia Marathon, Pennsylvania

A coworker from my school was there to run her first marathon. Three months prior to the event, I told her she could complete the marathon in 4 hours. I arranged for her to run with the 4:00 pacing group. Along the race route, I saw her and gave her a high five.

She was doing well with the 4:00 pacer and she actually finished 2 minutes ahead of the group. I finished at 3:45:19.

2004

1/18/2004 Houston Marathon, Texas

I unofficially paced someone. I was going for a best time of 3:35, but chose to help someone who needed lip balm. As I was running, I pulled out a tube of lip balm to apply it to my dry lips. The person next to me spoke up and said that she could use some lip balm as well. I handed it to her and she was very glad. I met my "lip balm buddy" at Mile 11 and found out that she was an active duty Marine. I ended up bringing her in at 3:45. I tried to share in her joy as she crossed the finish line, but my emotions were distant because I didn't achieve a PR (personal record). It was the least I could do for someone who protects our country in active service. It was a privilege, an honor, and a joy to help her.

3/07/2004 Little Rock Marathon, Arkansas's Race For Every Pace

I fell in love with Little Rock, Arkansas, home of the friendliest marathon. From the moment I landed at the airport, everyone I encountered was so friendly. I got to the Expo and was shocked (and pleasantly surprised) to find the Expo volunteers were even MORE friendly! On the day of the race I was going to pace myself, but at the 12th mile, I ran into a pacer and no longer wanted to run by myself. He was keeping a great pace and had 5 runners in his group. I asked him if I could run with him and he eagerly took me on. I was the only one who finished with the pacer, partly because of the hill at Mile 23! The pacer and I hugged at the finish line. I was sure that I wanted to pace the following year. Gina and Geneva were the race directors or the "CIC" (Chicks in Charge) and I met them at the finish line as well. I vowed to pace it every year! The pacer was on track for a finish time of 4 hours and we finished the marathon in 3:54:39, almost 6 minutes ahead of time because of me.

3/20/2004 Shamrock Sportsfest Marathon, Virginia Beach, Virginia

I met Diana Burton at the start line and we hit it off right away. She had some spark! I could tell by the New York City crown she had on her head. We chatted through the race and I found out that she was 10 years older than me. I couldn't believe it! I thought we were the same age. Although she was a veteran runner, I unofficially paced her. Virginia Beach became one of my favorite marathons, mostly because of Diana.

4/24/2004 Country Music Marathon, Nashville, Tennessee

Lynn Durham, a supervisor I knew from Christmas around the World, picked me up at the airport and I stayed with her. Lynn was not running in the marathon. As her husband Phil put it, "The only exercise Lynn gets is jumping to conclusions." Lynn dropped me at the marathon an hour before start time. Bad storms delayed things by 20 minutes and resulted in a disorganized start. There wasn't even time to get a jacket or put my drop bag in the assigned area. So with time being down to the wire, I ran into the hotel lobby and asked a hotel worker if he had a bag. Like a New York fashion designer, he fashioned a pseudo-jacket by cutting out neck and arm holes in a trash bag— "OOOO-LA-LAH!!!." Cutting edge fashion, but I was very appreciative and dry! My next mission was to secure my bag. I gave my drop bag to a spectator and asked him to put it in the storage truck under "B." I figured Truck B would be easy to remember, B for Bartoletti." He didn't speak any English, but the guy next to him did, and placed my bag in the truck. With no time to spare, I started the race. You've heard of the song, "Singing in the Rain?" Well, I was "Running in the Rain." It rained for an hour. Then the sun came out and the country musicians began playing along the race route to provide entertainment and musical encouragement. I finished the race in 3:53:19. I got my drop bag from Truck B (thank you, kind stranger). I called Lynn and then grabbed some nourishment and water. After that brief recharging, Lynn arrived. I put on my cowboy hat and we went to the Brad Paisley concert. I prepped for that, too. The lunch supervisor at McClellan had a Brad Paisley CD that she had let me borrow. So I listened, and was able to sing along at the concert!

5/30/2004 Vermont City Marathon, Vermont

When my sons were younger, we stayed at my friend, Margaret Ferguson's, house in Vermont on a ski trip. This time, I returned to Margaret's house with my friend, Susie. Saturday, before the marathon, we picnicked with Margaret's family at her dad's farm, complete with a pond! We ate dinner outside and chilled out before the big race day. I remember a big hill around Mile 19 where we met a group of drummers. They beat out a rhythm that helped me keep pace up that hill! I completed the marathon in 3:56:33.

6/06/2004 Rock and Roll Marathon, San Diego, California

This is another Train to End Stroke event and my favorite marathon. My son, David, 18 years old at the time, ran with me. We shared a hotel room and he was surprised to learn I was a snorer. "Mom, you didn't tell me that!" I was his unofficial pacer. At Mile 16, Susie was on the sideline. When David spotted her, he said, "I want to run with Susie." As a fellow Train to End Stroke trainer, it was her turn to be on the sidelines. The trainers take turns pacing and staying on the sidelines. Susie broke with tradition and cheerfully accepted David's invitation to run with him. Susie was in very good shape and wanted to run a mile with David. That mile proved to be refreshing for David and me. I remember that we got to mile 26 and I said, "We are almost there." David replied, "WE ARE NOT! We have .2 miles left." Lesson learned, next time I wouldn't say that! Immediately after, David got a tattoo on his ankle to commemorate the event. David plays keyboard in the band "The Werks" and provides vocals. His tattoo was in the shape of a guitar with the date 6/6/04 and 26.2. My reaction was mixed. I said, "Awww," but then the mom side of me kicked in and asked, "Where is "Mom" on your tattoo?" We shared a good laugh and David held his hand to his heart and told me that our day together was forever in his heart, which meant more to me than he could ever know. By the way, he got 4:36:35. What a time to beat, not due to the training! Fellow

David's First Marathon

Train to End Stroke participants remarked to David, "That's a fantastic time! You must have your mother's legs!"

8/15/2004 Humpy's Classic Marathon, Anchorage, Alaska

The day before, I went to the hotel concierge looking for something to do. He suggested a plane ride, so I did. I took the shuttle bus to the airstrip and along the way a fellow passenger recognized me from my Wheaties box. She was from the Ohio area. We quickly realized that her daughter and my son were good friends at Kent State. Who would have thought we'd meet on a shuttle bus in Alaska. As luck would have it, the sight-seeing group had one spot left for an extended excursion I had booked a shorter trip, so I took it. In fact, I sat next to the pilot and he was impressed to meet me. The band Styx had recently been on his plane and now he was excited to have me on board as well. The pilot landed in a rather remote spot. I had no camera, but the overwhelming scenery is forever in my mind. Later that afternoon, I took a multi-person kayak to see mighty glaciers. Pictures do not do justice to the majesty of Alaska, I was in awe. I also went to Denali which is the tallest land-based mountain in the North America. That evening, I went to the expo and afterwards had dinner at Humpy's Restaurant, sponsor of the marathon. A typical pre-race dinner includes pasta but when in Alaska, do as the Alaskans do. We had fish. The marathon went well and I finished in 3:52, followed by a bike ride for an additional 4 hours. I guess that fish dinner gave me oomph! During my bike ride, I encountered a mother and baby moose. I stopped and took a picture but was advised by the cyclist behind me to keep moving so the animals didn't charge me. I heeded the warning and biked a long, long, long way.

9/19/2004 Lewis and Clark Marathon, Bozeman, Montana

This time I've traveled to Montana. The scenery was beautiful and I hope to return one day. I arrived the day before the race and met Sam, the race director. Race directors are very busy people who are vital to the race going off as planned. Sam was no exception and I recognized that he could use some help. We coordinated the food and drinks, and I helped pass out the bibs to the participants. The course was all gravel and dirt and there was no shortage of hills. I wanted to encompass the whole race, the awesome snowcapped mountains, and the crystal blue, cloudless sky. I managed to finish at 3:55:48, which is a good finish time, and I HAD a great time! I learned a lot from Sam, which helped me to complete the next series of marathons.

10/31/2004 Marine Corps Marathon, Washington, D.C.

I paced 4:30 and finished at 4:29:45. Little did I know at the time, that I was about to tackle my first back-to-back marathons. My name had been drawn to run in the New York City Marathon the following week. Actually, it was two firsts for me. It would be the first of many times that I would run consecutive weekends and the first time that I would run the New York City Marathon. The next 20 years, I was pacing the New York City Marathon!.

Bozeman Marathon

11/07/2004 New York City Marathon

I finished in 4:03:15 which was awesome. I hadn't been confident that I could complete back-to-back marathons. My body actually felt good afterwards, which was somewhat confusing at the time. To cap it off, the race was spectacular, and I ran through all 5 boroughs of the city and got to stay with my cousins, Marty and Candy Monaco in Manhattan.

2005: (26 marathons)

1/3/05/2005 Las Vegas International Marathon, Nevada

My time was 3:56:44. Before the race, Susie and I walked the Vegas Strip. During the marathon the wind gusted at 60 miles an hour and blew over a Port-A-John with Susie inside. She was ahead of me, but I saw the aftermath. It wasn't until the finish line that she told me her harrowing tale. After the race, I wanted to hug her but decided to wait until AFTER she took her shower!

On Mile 15 I was tired from fighting the wind and struggling to not get blown down. I thought about drafting: running behind another person with very little space in between. You expend a little less energy. Drafting is not permitted in Triathlons. Participants would get a yellow warning flag. After receiving two yellow flags, the participant gets a red flag at which time they are sent to the tent for a time penalty. It's the runner's equivalent of being sent to the principal's office. In a regular marathon, drafting is permitted with some understandings. It is best to ask the runner you want to draft if they would be ok with it. If not asked, some runners will turn around and shoot some looks at the person drafting. So to be courteous, I asked a tall guy, "Would you mind if I ran behind you and draft?." He said, "Sure." That was nice of him. That's a miracle. I drafted for 10 miles. It was awesome. By Mile 25, I went to his side and we talked to each other. He was a nice guy because he didn't have to do that and it made an impact on me as a future pacer. When I became an official pacer, I took note of the wind. If it was windy, I would try to place the stronger runners toward the front and the novices were encouraged to draft behind them. Runners helping runners to achieve a common goal, the finish line, which we crossed at 3:56:44.

2/27/2005 New Orleans Mardi Gras Marathon

I unofficially paced someone. She was going for 3:50 and we kept passing each other along the way. At four miles, she spoke to me. "You are consistent in your pace. I hurt my arm two weeks ago and this was going to be my Boston qualifier, but I'm in pain. Can you help me?" I gladly stepped up to the plate. Every mile we kept a steady pace. I told her jokes, discussed my life, and she didn't have to talk at all. We came in at 3:46—a Boston Marathon qualifying time for her age bracket! She hugged me at the finish. We took a picture together. This race would mark my last unofficial pace!

I "OFFICIALLY" had the pacing bug! I went about figuring out how to be an official pacer. I contacted the race director for the New Jersey Marathon to ask if they needed at 4:00 pacer. I also contacted the race director for the Oklahoma City Marathon, Mark Bravo, who authorized me to pace 4:00.

5/09-10/2005 TOSRV "Tour of the Sciota River Valley", Columbus, Ohio.

The nation's largest bicycle touring weekend fell on Mother's Day Weekend. Friday night, I picked up my packet. For $10, I stayed overnight at the YMCA in the sleeping bag I brought along. I awoke in the wee hours to meet the dawn and begin my ride. I stored my sleeping bag and duffle bag in the truck provided by the race, and I got right to it. The tour takes two days, each day is 105 miles. Portions were flat, others hilly. I stopped four times the first day at volunteer stations for water, Gatorade, fig bars, and such. I hit the final stop of the day at 3:30 and was glad to see that truck with my stuff. A gymnasium floor is where I would spend the night. NOT the plush mattress that one would hope for after biking for 105 miles, but it would have to do. That evening, I attended Mass at a local church and a pasta dinner. The volunteers are always top-notch, but these volunteers were outstanding. Sunday morning, I woke up early and started the return trip, which seemed to be a little faster than the day before.

As a side note, three years later I was speaking with my students about biking the TOSRV. One of my 5th grade students, a boy, excitedly blurted out, "My family is going there too!" It warmed my heart to see the sparkle in his eyes as he talked about tackling the TOSRV with his family.

4/17/2005 New Jersey Marathon

I was an OFFICIAL pacer at 4:00! There were about 10 people in my time group and I was able to bring in 4 or 5 of those runners. We finished at 3:59:58. It was a fantastic time capped off by having so many of my pace group finish with me!

4/24/2005 Oklahoma City Memorial Marathon, Oklahoma

Sadness had torn through Oklahoma in 1995 due to the worst devastating terrorist bombing in American history. I stopped at one of the booths where victims' pictures and bios were displayed. They were encouraging runners to dedicate the marathon to a victim or victims. I carefully looked at each picture and read the stories, but was having a difficult time selecting someone. Next to me was a teenaged girl who saw me looking at the pictures. This young lady approached and through tears began to tell me that her father was killed in the bombing. She asked if I would be willing to dedicate my race to his memory. I accepted this honor. She hugged me then and again at the finish line. I wore a shirt with her father's picture as I crossed the finish line.

7/03/2005 Gold Coast Marathon, Queensland, Australia

I had become pen pals with Cathy Love, from Australia, during our freshman year of high school, and we remained friends. She offered to have me stay with her for the Gold Coast Marathon. Cathy worked for an airline in Australia and lived in Sydney, so she picked me up at the airport. The day after my arrival, we climbed the Sydney Harbor Bridge, is the largest bridge in the world. Atop it, we had a breathtaking 360-degree view of Sydney Harbor. It took an hour and a half to complete the climb. Later, at the Wildlife Sydney Zoo, I got to see my first koalas and kangaroos! We went to the Sydney Opera House, magnificent with its sparkling, sail-like design. I was also eager to see the beautiful Botanical Gardens. Even though it was raining, I ran to the spot where the Olympics were held the year prior as it was only a mile from Cathy's house. Other people were walking around the Olympics stadium and one mother told me that her son, who was seven years old, hadn't seen the sun since he had been born. Apparently it had been rainy and cloudy for a long time. Cathy was working, so I took a bus ride out to the winery. I didn't want to bike in the rain. I sampled wines from four different wineries, so I guess it was a good thing I didn't ride my bike. The rain had diminished to a sprinkle so I went to Bondi Beach. It was too cold to swim. I had been thinking about my Dad as I strolled through a little beachfront shop. I saw tea samples and bought some for him immediately since he had a cup of tea every day, a bottle of wine for me, tea for Dad. The marathon was about an hour or two from Sydney and Cathy had a free flight, but she had to sit in the jump seats. I was way back in the cabin, but I felt so proud to have her with me. We went to the Expo. I was pacing 4:15 so I got my balloons and was told to pin them to the back of my bra. Typically, during a pre-race party, the runners are offered pasta for the carbs. However, the pacers at this race were going to a pizza party. I was nervous about having pizza prior to the race and even more leery when I saw it was pineapple and ham, It was delicious and the company of the pacers was outstanding.

The morning of the race went smoothly until I realized that I had printed a pace band, but totally forgot the race was in kilometers! I asked around if anyone had a pace band in kilometers and found a fellow runner who offered to stay with me. The race started and "bra balloons" were clunking around and whacking other runners in the face. So, I held the strings of the balloons for the entirety of the race. This particular course had a turn-around which was marked by pylons three feet high. Note the height. One unfortunate guy did not note the height and ran groin-first into the pylon. I yelled, "Are you ok?" and the poor fellow squeaked out a pained, "Yes." I saw him about 5 minutes later when he wound up next to me but a safe distance from those pylons!

My idea of a pacing is to help runners cross the finish line by doing whatever I can to keep their spirits up. On the second half, when things started to get a little boring, I started telling jokes from the Laffy Taffy candies. My pace group chimed in with their own jokes which got us through to the ocean view. We were enthused by the beach and even more enthused at crossing the finish line! I finished at 4:14:12. 4:15 was my pacing time!

7/20/2005 Grandfather Mountain Marathon, Boone, North Carolina

One of America's toughest mountain marathons has been held each year since 1969 during the Grandfather Mountain

Highland Games, one of the largest Scottish Games in America. The sound of bagpipes was amazing. The racetrack was the finishing spot with an estimated 5,000 spectators watching me and I finished at 4:47:31.

10/08/2005 Hartford Marathon, Hartford, Connecticut

It had been raining the night before and ALL night long. The US Postal System has the motto, "neither rain, nor snow, nor hail, nor dead of night will keep us from our appointed rounds." My marathon motto was the same as Connecticut would prove. I was supposed to pace 4:15 and was given an enormous sign that I was supposed to hold to alert members of the 4:15 group of our location in the starting area. Rain tends to deter people from marathons. It's hard enough to run a marathon with wet socks and squishy shoes, but low spectator turnout with no one to cheer runners along is extra difficult. I got to the finish line and my ride was waiting to take me to the airport. I crossed the finish line at 4:14, as a 4:15 pacer. As soon as I crossed the finish line, I hopped in the car and headed to the airport for my flight to Chicago. Yes, I was running the Chicago marathon the next day.

I boarded the plane and the flight attendant was somewhat bewildered when I walked onboard with my bunny ears, bib, and soaking wet t-shirt. Perhaps she mistook me for a Playboy bunny with the wet t-shirt and bunny ears, who knows? She asked about my wet outfit and I told her I had just completed a marathon in the rain and was off to my next one in Chicago. She offered me a cup of hot coffee and my seatmate offered a jacket. Whenever I meet strangers, they turn out to be as helpful as can be. Once we landed, Don Pattison, good friend, picked me up and noticed my squishing, soggy running shoes. He offered to put my only pair of shoes in the dryer and I agreed. However, if there's one thing I've learned since then is that newspaper is the way to go. To all of the runners out there with wet shoes, crumple up newspaper and stuff it in. Your shoes will be dry in no time without the threat of shrinkage.

12/03/2005 St. Jude Memphis Marathon, Tennessee

I paced 4:30 and came in at 4:29:03. After the race, a group of pacers went out for dinner. I got up from the table to go to the restroom and didn't notice a step down. I twisted my right ankle. I was able to play it off because no one saw it happen. When I got back to my hotel room, I began to feel it. I took off my sock and a bump had already formed. I grabbed the ice bucket and limped my way to the ice machine. The ice calmed it down I thought I was going to be good to go.

12/11/2005 Honolulu Marathon, Hawaii

This marathon completed my goal of running a marathon in all 50 states in two years (2004-2005). I was feeling good at the beginning, though my right ankle wasn't as good as gold. My goal was to finish in under 4 hours. The sports drink I had was terrible. I started to notice some pain in my stomach. I had to get to a bathroom—FAST! Twice, actually. The pit stops took about 10 minutes but I felt much better. However, when I crossed the finish line I was disappointed to learn that I finished in 4:14. I was elated to have run in all 50 states though!

When I returned from Hawaii, I went to my job at the elementary school. We had been working up to running a mile. The students were excited to run in their first marathon as part of the Kids of Steel program in May, 2006 so I ran with each grade level during their P.E. class. We ran laps in the gym; twelve laps to make a mile. Each time I rounded the corner, I hurt. I took a look at my right ankle and saw blue marks on my skin— Oh no! I called the podiatrist and was able to be seen right away. He took an X-ray and he said the same thing— "Oh No!" Diagnosis: torn tendon. Plan: surgery. My mind was racing, even if my body couldn't at that moment.

2006: (20 marathons)

1/2/2006 I had surgery on my right ankle. The doctor was pleased with the results and in 2 months, I'd be back to running marathons.

The problem was, I was already scheduled to pace and run in several marathons. I had an obligation…and a bum ankle. My flight to Disney World was booked for January 5th. I was determined to do it—but how? I reached out to my friend, Carol Lee and she offered me her aunt's wheelchair. I was extremely thankful to borrow it, but unfortunately it had a bad wheel. I guess it kind of matched my "bad wheel." Quite the pair! My next move was to call and notify the pacing group that there was a change of plans. I started rehabbing right away by ordering and using a sit-up machine, getting on my balance ball and bicycling with my left leg only. My son, David, was living with me then and said, "Don't worry Mom, if you can't run, you have something else to do. Teach." I returned to work as a P.E. teacher in a wheelchair.

1/5/2006 I manage to get myself to the airport. "Airport Services" helped me reach the gate. I only had one backpack no bags to check in.

1/6/2006 I went to the Expo in a wheelchair. I posted a sign on the back asking for help with the race. I knew a lot of people there and they said, "Good job!" and if they happened to see me along the route, they would push me.

1/07/2002 I was scheduled to run a half marathon. I got to the start line in my chair and began talking to a man next to me. He and his brother were Notre Dame alum so he felt like he had a connection with me because my father, sister, and brothers had all gone to Notre Dame. Of these two brothers, one was an experienced runner and the other a first-timer. The seasoned runner pushed me and the novice was having a rough time. Both brothers made it. We were all happy for each other. But I wasn't out of the woods yet, I had a FULL marathon the next day.

1/8/2006 Disney World Marathon, Orlando, Florida

I got to the start line with no helpers. I asked several runners for help. My first helper asked other runners if they would push me for one mile each. They did it! However, at Mile 13, I didn't have anyone to help me. I saw 3 people wearing pirate hats. I spoke up, "ARRRGG mateys, would ye mind helping out a peg leg pirate?" Not only did they take turns pushing me the rest of the way, they also gave me a pirate hat because I was chilly and they were too hot. Along the way, I learned my band of pirates was from Ontario, Canada and that one of the pirates was going for a personal record, of six hours. The pirates continued to push my wheelchair, taking turns. Donna Lockhart, the "head pirate," and I bonded and continue to keep in touch for years after. The pirate trying for a PR took her turn pushing my wheelchair as well. To her delight, she found that pushing my chair was actually relaxing and helped to keep her in a steady rhythm. In fact, she offered to push me the rest of the way! Our band of pirates came in at 5:49:09—a new personal record for Donna Lockhart!

3/52/2006 Little Rock Marathon, Arkansas' Race for every Pace

I was still in a wheelchair and made it to the finish line without any helpers. My arm muscles felt every mile of it. Thirteen miles in, I saw Don Pattison from Chicago and called out, "Hey, look at me." Don responded, "Are you kidding me?" He offered to push me the rest of the way. I decided to let him push me and I came in at 6:08. (Thank you very much Don!!)

5/28/2006 Buffalo Marathon, New York

I met Jim Moran at the marathon Expo. I mentioned that I brought a bike to cycle in Niagara Falls the day after the race. He said his friend, Les, also cycled a lot, and lived only a 5 minute walk from Niagara Falls. When I met Les, Jim introduced me as having been on the Wheaties box. It validated me as a triathlete, and Les said he would be delighted to have me as a guest. Les had an interesting story. He had been hit by a large tow truck while riding his bike in June 2000. He was training for the Swiss Alpine Marathon in Switzerland. His bike was broken in half, but his body was even more battered. His life-threatening injuries included a shattered left leg, puncture wounds, broken ribs and a lacerated aorta that required emergency surgery. That surgery left him without the use of one vocal cord. The loss of Les's voice would later bond us when I suffered my stroke and wasn't speaking. I asked Les how he stayed strong throughout his ordeal and he said, "Staying positive, keeping my faith and being surrounded by great family and friends helped me get through this challenge in my life." These words brought me great comfort and strength after my stroke 15 years later.

After the marathon, I went to Les' house to stay the night. I met Peggy, his wife, and she made dinner. The next day, we cycled to Niagara on the Lake and back. In the middle of our ride, I spotted a shoe store. I decided to make a quick pit stop and take advantage of the great Canadian discounts. During our bike ride, I learned that Les was a retired physical education teacher. He said he was working at Brock University. We decided that he would come to my school and teach some dance workshops to my classes. (I was excited when our plan actually happened and Les came to Pittsburgh the following year.)

While staying at Les and Peggy's, I walked to St. Patrick's Church and met Rev. Gerard Power, who was a good friend of Les and Peggy's.

10/22/2006 Chicago Marathon

I paced the 4:30 group with Jerry Vondruska. We had met at the Chicago marathon the previous year and stayed in touch with one another. I came in at 4:29:51 pacing 4:30.

11/11/2006 Mother Road 100 Marathon Route 66, Oklahoma City to Tulsa, Oklahoma

I call this my "famous race." I got 1st place with the next closest female competitor three and a half hours behind me! I was 1st place at Mile 50 among both the men and women, but I had to go the bathroom. Someone, told me I should just tinkle on the side of the road, but I opted to run a side road to find a gas station bathroom. I had to enter the gas station, and ask for the key. All the while, I hear the tick-tock, tick-tock of my 1st place time. By

Les Potapczyk and Me

Jerry Vondruska and me after Chicago Marathon

the time I ran a half-down mile back to the course, I had fallen to 3rd place. Two men were ahead of me. Then at Mile 73, a passing motorist threw an egg out of his window. I had never experienced such a thing! I saw something whiz past my head and as I ducked down, I realized it was an egg. I told the workers at the next aid station about the experience and they were as shocked as I was. As they got in their vehicle to try to find the perpetrator's, I vividly remembered the black sedan.

At Mile 85, my friend Susie and I met up and ran together. By this time, it was midnight. From out of nowhere, a dog came lunging at us from out of the darkness. I was scared. Susie said for me to run ahead and she would calm the dog and take care of it. I got to Mile 96 and I couldn't see. My contacts were blurry. I asked Susie to go to the finish line and she said, "Okay." I was wrong. I needed her for my "sight." We finished at a hamburger joint. I finished in third place. The number 2 female was three and a half hours behind me. It was a learning experience. I was given a piece of asphalt from Mother Road Route 66!

Mother Road Ultra Tee Shirt front.

Mother Road Ultra Tee Shirt back.

Mother Road Ultra Finish Line

2007: (26 marathons this year)

01/28/2007 Miami Marathon, Florida

I was pacing the rather large 4:30 group. I came up with a cheer for the completion of each mile. "4:30 ROCKS!." Each mile, I'd cheer, "4:30 ROCKS MILE 2," "4:30 ROCKS MILE 3," etc. Janine, from Chicago, ran next to me and she told me how she met her fiancé, now husband, through speed dating. Janine ran with our group for 20 miles and began to feel as though she wanted to back off. The marathon was taking its toll. For the next few miles, I talked to her. I told her maybe I need to speed date and find my one true love, who would hopefully be a pilot to fly me to future marathons. It became clear that she wouldn't finish at 4:30 so she made the decision to back off, but my persuasion as a pacer remained with her. My large group of 4:30 started to lag back, but Janine was there to take them under her wing. She carried on the tradition of cheering, "4:30 Rocks" at every mile marker. If others from the original 4:30 Rocks group began to lag, my protégé was there to catch them. I waited for her at the finish line and gave her a big hug! Janine also told me about a friend of hers who was looking for someone to pace her. Janine saw me as a perfect match for Gayle, who always went out too fast. If Gayle was to make her goal Boston qualifying time, she would need me.

3/04/2007 Little Rock Marathon, Arkansas' Race for every Pace

I had already qualified for Boston so this was my chance to help others do the same. I was pacing the 4:00 group and tried to get to know them better. I asked if there were any runners about to run their first marathon and we clapped for them. Next, I asked if anyone was qualifying for Boston and Miriam was one of the three runners who held her hand up high. We lost two of them as we headed towards Mile 20. Mile 20 contained a daunting hill so I held my hand on Miriam's back as we began our ascent. She was scared, but I remained calm and confident that we were getting to Boston! At Mile 25, I looked over at Miriam and said, "Go ahead, you can do it!." It was an emotional reunion at the finish line. Miriam finished a little before my 4:00 pace time which gave her time to collect her husband and greet me as I brought the group in at 3:58:17. It was a proud moment for all of us!

7/27/2007 San Francisco Marathon, San Francisco, California

It was my 100th marathon and I was wearing bib number 100! I came in at 5:14:31 and was pacing 5:15. At Mile 9, one of my pacing group fell down and cut his knee so I got a Band Aid for him. Five people were left by Mile 20 and we had just passed a big hill. I brought in my group of 5 and then circled back around to try to help others finish. People recognized me by my bunny-eared hat and remarked that they had just seen me. I repeated this a total of 5 times, looping back and bringing in more runners.

10/07/2007 Medtronic Twin Cities Marathon, Minneapolis to St. Paul, Minnesota

I was a pacer. I ran in this race in 2006 and I remembered that many of the spectators had dogs with them. Some people count sheep, my group decided to count dogs! The runner next to me kept count and the other runners would chime in when they spotted a dog. Dog counting turned out to be a great distraction. The crowd was entertained as well. I shook the spectator's hand of the 100th dog we counted. He asked if I had a prize for him, but I told him I wasn't carrying dog treats or a medal so I offered him a gel. We shared a good laugh. I was half-way through when I asked my group if they wanted to play a guessing game. Everyone agreed. At 13.1, we were up to 225 dogs so I polled the group and asked them how many dogs they thought we'd tally by the finish line. Everyone took turns yelling out a guess, "300," "425," and even "600!" At about our 400th dog, we realized that the spectators were moving position along the race route and we had been counting many of the same dogs twice! Although our tabulation was not quite accurate, we counted 435 dogs. Maybe next time we should have sensors on the dogs as well as the runners.

12/09/2007 Dallas White Rock Marathon, Texas

I paced 4:30. It was at this race that I met Maneesha who was assigned to be my roommate for the two nights in town. Maneesha was from California and was pacing the 5:30 group. We hung with each other for the entire weekend and bonded. On Sunday, we talked about the Badwater ultramarathon because Maneesha's brother, David, was very interested in the event. It's a Big West Coast invitational. Not everybody can run in Badwater. I was selected because of my 1st place finish in a 100 mile ultramarathon, a full three and a half hours ahead of the next closest woman. I remembered overhearing about Badwater the previous summer at Grandma's Marathon. The seed had been planted, and once I placed 1st in the Ultra, I knew I had a chance at Badwater. I filled out my application, but I wouldn't hear until January. A few of my runner buddies stepped up to offer to pace me in portions of Badwater, including Maneesha and Jerry. Jerry Vondruska was my best friend from Chicago. We had paced the 4:30 group in Chicago year after year. He and his brother would be part of my pace team. Other friends would generously offer to pace me through Badwater. I knew things were changing very abruptly as I began to generate my Badwater team. My friend, Susie Albert, also volunteered to pace me.

2008: (27 marathons)

3/02/2008 Little Rock Marathon, Arkansas' Roce for every Pace

Remember Miriam from last year? I ran into her at the Expo. They asked the pace team to step forward to the front of the room. When the question and answer time came, Miriam raised her hand and asked if I remembered her. Tears began to well up in my eyes. She told me that she successfully completed Boston in 2007. At the time of the Expo, I didn't know that I'd be pacing her daughter as she ran her first marathon. As we got to the starting line, I asked if any person was running in their first marathon. A young girl raised her hand and said she'd be running in her first half marathon, which I was also pacing. She meekly asked,

"Do you know Miriam." I said that Miriam was my shining star! The young lady said that she was Miriam's daughter—another generation of runners stepping up to the starting line.

3/15/2008 Shamrock Marathon, Virginia Beach, Virginia

As part of the registration fee, the runners were provided with a "Shamrock Marathon" t-shirt. It quickly became one of my favorites because it commemorated my race with my friend, Diana. Tuck that shirt away in your memory, because it will play an important part in 2011. At the finish line, we were each given two drink tickets. I gave mine away, but I got a bowl of chili and danced with my new-found friends in the pacing group.

4/21/2008 Boston Marathon, Massachusetts

There is a term called "out and back." A group of 9 of us lined up at the FINISH line at 6:00 a.m., and we ran towards the START. The spectators were bewildered, to say the least. A few of them questioned why we were going backwards. I couldn't hold back my sense of humor. I told them, "Just a minute, I'm on my way to the Boston Marathon." They laughed and so did I! Our group of backwards runners were "big time" runners. I knew I was running with the "Big Dogs!" We chatted as we ran and I came to find out that I would be seeing a few of them in Badwater in July. I listened very carefully to their advice about Badwater. Runners are very helpful individuals.

I crossed the "START" line (aka the finish line) in 3:51. I spent the next 40 minutes chatting with people who were running the official marathon. They, too, were baffled that I had just run the course in reverse and was preparing to start it. To tell the truth, I don't remember much of the specifics of those 40 minutes because I was so excited to run Boston. Running the course backwards was an uplifting experience because the other runners were so respected in the running world.

My official Boston Marathon finish time was 4:00:26, which was exceptional given that I had run the complete marathon in reverse only hours before. But, nothing could quite prepare me for Badwater which was only a few months away.

Boston Marathon Out and Back Group

5/24/2008 Bayshore, Michigan Marathon

I met Gayle McMurry for the first time. Her good friend Janine Gauthier, whom I paced in Miami in January of 2007, asked me to come to pace Gayle, who wanted to qualify for Boston. I drove to Traverse City over night from Pittsburg and arrived the morning of the Bayshore Marathon. I met Gayle and off we went. She needed to run 4:15 to qualify. Janine ran with us. Gayle started to go ahead of me about 2 miles into the race. I yelled for her to come back to me and run alongside me. My experience told me that if she over exerted her energy too early in the race, she may ultimately run out of energy and end with 4:25 or longer. Gayle's husband, Mike, was stationed as a spectator at Mile 20 where he greeted Gayle with a look of surprise and pride. She was doing it!!! He paced Gayle for a half mile and that was exactly what she needed to boost her morale. They parted ways, but agreed to meet up at the finish line. True to his word, Mike was waiting for us as we crossed the finish line. He hugged and kissed her, and his look of pride said it all. She had qualified for Boston! The marathon finished on the local high school track. We finished in 4:13:49. I clapped and cheered around the track to all the spectators "This is Gayle. She's going to Boston!" Gayle offered to pay me for pacing her for a Boston qualifying time, but I declined the money. Instead, she made a very generous donation to Challenged Athletes Foundation in my honor.

After the marathon I made the trip to stay with my Mom in my childhood home for a few days.

School was out for the summer. Without teaching five days a week, I could focus on training and conditioning for Badwater. My friend, Jerry, suggested I change up my usual exercise regimen and add jump rope and sauna, which simulated the heat I would be running through for 135 miles. Even as an experienced runner, I was very nervous. Running is not just a race against a clock, for me, it is driven by my internal ambition and fear of letting myself and other people down. A lot was riding on Badwater. I began to select marathons that provided an extra challenge, including Cleveland, where I ran a 4:13 marathon on Sunday and another 20 miles bright and early Monday morning. Cleveland was on the heels of the Cincinnati "Flying Pig" marathon the week before. These events, plus the Oklahoma City marathon on 4/27/2008, where I paced the 5 hour group, were preparing my body for what was to come—if that was possible.

Me, Jannie Gauthier Mullady, and Gayle McMurry

7/14-16/2008 Badwater Ultramarathon, Death Valley to Mt.Whitney, California

This was it. I was one of 130 runners trying to beat Badwater. I arrived in California, the day before the Sunday race and stayed with Maneesha overnight. Maneesha drove me and the rest of my team to Furnace Creek the following day. I had a wonderful team of people, each of whom had a big role to play: Jerry, Susie, Reagan, Bryan, Lori, and Maneesha were my crew. Jerry was voted to be the leader because he had done this before. He was in charge of charting my miles, electrolyte intake and time of day. Susie was my best friend and did a great job pacing me during the race. Reagan was an excellent masseur and he gave me a full-body massage the night before and encouraged me a lot during the race. Bryan, Jerry's brother, and Lori did a lot behind the scenes. Maneesha was the official hand-wipe passer-outer.

My team was very dedicated and devoted. They paid for their own traveling expenses and incidentals. They took a lot of the burden of planning. As a group, they decided to divide and conquer, each taking charge of a different part. Jerry had a big job! At Mile 26, I was feeling very sick with a stomach ache and nausea. Barely a quarter of the way through the race, I had no idea how I was going to finish. The team realized that I had not been

Badwater

Dean Karnazes and me running Badwater

receiving enough hydration. It was almost too late, but Jerry set up a tarp and sponge bathed me. He kept the Gatorade and water coming and I felt alive again!

I knew there was a pool coming up at Mile 60 and I desperately wanted to take a dip and cool off as the temperature was well over 100 degrees. I was running through the desert when I saw the pool ahead like a mirage. I arrived and submerged my body, but quickly realized that the water was hot. I swam a quick lap and then got out of there. So much for a cool, refreshing dip!

Looking back on the whole experience, it was a whirlwind. To get me through, I dedicated each mile to a different person. Since there are 141 miles in Badwater, my pacing team kept track of each mile's dedication. My sons, David and Michael, got miles 21 and 23, 121 and 123 to mark their ages. The whole time I ran those miles, I thought about them growing up. That provided me with mental stimulation to distract from the physical strain. Similarly, I dedicated miles 9 and 109 to my parents in honor of the nine people in our family. Mile 4 was dedicated to my sister, Anne, whose favorite number was 4. Mile 66 was dedicated to my dear friend and fellow runner, Mark Bravo.

Badwater National Anthem

It took me 35 hours to complete the race, so the whole time I was debating to sleep or not to sleep. I decided not to sleep, to just keep going. At one point, I did decide to treat myself to a shower. However, sleep deprivation was getting to all of us, and my team's sense of humor got a little mixed up. They decided to put a snake in my shoe while I was taking a shower and took a picture. Thankfully, I didn't see the picture until the next day! Otherwise, I would have just run barefoot through the desert for the rest of the race. These are just a few of many perils you face when running Badwater!

Around 2 a.m., I saw bats circling around in the sky. At least they weren't vultures.

With just five miles left in the race, I was walking up the hill and saw Brian sitting on a toilet that my team had brought out from the van. They were trying to keep my sense of humor for those last few miles as I climbed up Mount Whitney to the finish line! I came in at 35:47:31. I had a 13th place finish. My team and I even managed to smile and pose for a picture at the finish line.

Badwater Finish Line

Badwater Belt Buckle

2009: (24 marathons)

5/01/2009 Kids of Steel Program

The Pittsburgh Marathon did not exist for a few years. Patrice Matamorus took over as race director and the Pittsburgh Marathon was alive and well again!

Patrice was a fantastic and dedicated race director. She invited me to an exclusive dinner where I met Meb Keflezighi, first place winner in the previous year's New York City Marathon. I could tell immediately why everyone loved Meb. He had a great personality and was down to earth. Patrice and I had been building a program for youth runners in Pittsburgh. We encouraged elementary school students in the district where I taught P.E. to try running by starting with a quarter mile. Each time we practiced, we'd increase the increments and played music to keep them going. I ran right alongside them. By the time of the by-invitation-only dinner, my students had reached 26 miles! The students took their training very seriously. They completed a training schedule both during P.E. and

Patrice Matamoros, Pittsburgh Marathon Race Director

at home. Although the marathon training was not required to pass their P.E. course, the participation rate was unbelievable. I had 76 students turn in their permission slips and train. And there you have it, the Kids of Steel program was born!

SOUTH HILLS RECORD | MAY 19, 2011 | PAGE 15

PHOTO/STEPHANIE HACKE

McCLELLAN ELEMENTARY School physical education teacher Marie Bartoletti, center, won the American Hellenic Foundation of Western Pennsylvania's Pheidippides award for her contributions to the Dick's Sporting Goods Pittsburgh Marathon. She is surrounded by Kids Marathon participants, from left, Lily Rockwell, Faith Rockwell, Sydney Moran and Tito Matulula.

Teacher helps students put best feet forward

BY STEPHANIE HACKE
STAFF WRITER

Running alongside their best friends, brothers, sisters, dads, moms, classmates and teachers was fun.

And as they huff and puff for air, with rosy red cheeks, they know what they are doing is not only good for the soul, but their bodies as well.

"It's a good way to get exercise," said McClellan Elementary fourth-grader Sydney Moran, 10. "It's important to me that we got fit while doing this."

McClellan physical education teacher Marie Bartoletti once again this year, for the second straight year, inspired a large number of her students to get fit by running in the Pittsburgh Kids of Steel marathon.

More than 120 out of 290 students Bartoletti teaches signed up for the event this year, up from the 68 who completed the race last year. While students completed one mile of the race Saturday, they've spent the last several weeks running – one to two miles at a time – to complete their own McClellan Elementary School marathon of 26.2 miles.

Motivating students to run isn't Bartoletti's only feat. The elementary school teacher has completed 204 marathons across the world, many of which she has served as a pace leader.

And no matter where she goes or what city she's racing, Bartolleti always is singing the praises of the Pittsburgh Marathon, she said.

"I want everyone to get involved," Bartoletti said. "I think it's fun."

For her efforts and contributions to the Dick's Sporting Goods Pittsburgh Marathon and "in recognition of the endurance, strength and the triumph of the human spirit," Bartoletti on Saturday was given the American Hellenic Foundation of Western Pennsylvania's Pheidippides award.

"It makes me feel like I'm trying to make a difference in people's lives," she said. "It's an honor."

Bartoletti participates in marathons for the enjoyment, she said.

"It's healthy. It's good exercise," Bartoletti said.

As she paces each mile, the woman who wears a unique decorative hat for each race chats with those around her to keep them motivated and distracted.

"I'm educating people," Bartoletti said. "I can tell them everything that I did wrong so they don't do the same thing."

In each race she completes, every mile is dedicated to someone. Many races, in part or whole, Bartoletti has ran in honor of Kayla Rush, a Pleasant Hills resident and McClellan student who died in August after a two and a half year battle with osteosarcoma.

Students at McClellan ran this year's race in Kayla's honor, adorning "Kayla's Brigade" bracelets around their wrists or ankles. Her brother, Nicolas, a kindergarten student at McClellan, also participated in the race with his friends, Bartoletti said.

"She was just a great little girl," Bartoletti said. "She was positive and never complaining."

Students also wore their gold tie dye, PTA-donated McClellan Elementary T-shirts in the race.

"It's really cool when you're down there and everyone knows who you are," Bartoletti said.

"I am excited about everything that I do," Bartoletti said. "A lot of people tell me that I'm like the Energizer bunny."

The McClellan kids enjoyed their time running the 25.2 miles around the community, mostly at South Park or the Thomas Jefferson High School track, or in physical

Teacher Inspires

Tempo

Teacher inspires others to be active

CONTINUED FROM PAGE 15

education class and recess time at their school, Bartoletti said.

"It's motivational for he kids. It gets them ictive," Bartoletti said.

Parents and siblings ere inspired to run with ie McClellan students.

Even students, some eschoolers, who do not tend McClellan ran the ce with the group. This ır, 80 students from asant Hills Middle ool also participated in marathon.

The kids who didn't do

PHOTO/STEPHANIE HACKE

Teacher Inspires

Teacher Inspires

Meb Keflezighi and me hugging

Meb Keflezighi and me running with Kids of Steel

Meb Keflezighi and me at VIP Dinner

8,000 children participating in the Kids of Steel program! At dinner that night, a bunch of us were socializing, and Patrice mentioned the Kids of Steel program to Meb. The Kids of Steel marathon would be held the following day, Saturday, and Meb volunteered to run with the kids. (Update-in 2018, there were 8,000 kids participating!)

8/08/2009 South Bend, Indiana

It was only about 2 weeks after my Dad passed away. I had just completed a 100 mile race and my brother, Tom, invited me to run a 10K with him in South Bend. My bib number was 37, our Dad's football jersey number at Notre Dame. Sibling rivalry kicked in as Tom and I briefly bickered about who would get to wear Dad's number. I ended up with 37 and Tom wore 38. There were no "givesies-backsies" because the bib is also imprinted with the runner's name.

8/18/2009 Pittsburgh, Pennsylvania

As a trainer with Fleet Feet, I was training adults at all stages of running expertise for an upcoming 5K. This is part of my passion, connecting with runners of all different speeds, stamina, and body type. This group was diverse as well. One of the novices,

Brother Tom and me

Me, Roy Pirrung, Brad Logan, and Jessica Etchen (Lyons) on a training run

Running with Dennis Schmatz in the Baltimore marathon

Brad Logan, was unwavering in his desire to complete his first 5K. Brad recently contacted me and told me that I was a big motivator in his quest to stay healthy. Since his first 5K, he has run full marathons. I had the pleasure of running alongside him in his first full one in Erie, PA in 2009. Roy Pirrung, a well-known ultramarathon runner, happened to be visiting me in Pittsburgh and decided to come along with us for our training run. Running with Roy and me built up Brad's confidence as a runner.

10/10/2009 Baltimore Marathon, Maryland

When I landed at the airport, I quickly learned how serious the fans of the Baltimore Ravens were! I happened to be wearing a Steelers shirt ("Big Ben's" jersey) and I was met with a chorus of boos! I was a proud Pittsburgher and held my head high! I knew I was staying with someone, a pacer, but I didn't know who. Pacers are a special breed who look out for one another. Even though I didn't know the name yet, I knew that as a fellow pacer it would work out fine! I was pacing 5 hours for my "pacee" Dennis Schmatz. I felt like a runway model with my pacing outfit and custom couture balloon hat!

10/11/2009 Chicago, Marathon, Illinois

You read that correctly, it is not a typo. Following the Baltimore Marathon, Don Pattison picked me up and we headed to Chicago where I paced the 4:30 group with a finish time of 4:29:55!! Not bad for the second marathon in 2 days! Don and I had a great time together at the pasta dinner and he was there at the start line with his crazy hat rooting for me.

12/13/2009 Dallas White Rock Marathon, Texas

I paced 5:00 and came in at 4:59:17 (can't get much closer than that!). I met Cathy Ozeroglu around Mile 5 or 6. Her friend had to quit the race at Mile 3 due to knee pain, and Cathy was on her own. Cathy spotted a woman carrying a sign with a group of runners following her. That woman was ME! Cathy had never run with a pacer. She never even knew such a thing existed. It was her third marathon. Cathy would later tell me that I was distracting her, but in a GOOD way. Before she knew it, we were at Mile 13 and she said she was feeling great. Between Miles 13 and 20, I began singing with the group, specifically the song "This Little Light of Mine." Cathy found herself running next to me at Mile 18. But the biggest challenge came around Mile 20 when the course began to go uphill. I sensed the group dwindling and losing energy. As the leader, I encouraged those that could, to go ahead and "break free." Several members of the original group were behind, but still following me and my sign. I had to do something to re-energize the group so I yelled out, "Hey, let's do the ABC's of marathon running." I got a few bewildered looks, but soon everyone in the group was joining in.

A Achievement
B Bravery
C Courage…..
D Determination

Soon we were to the letter Z. Zebras! They can't do a marathon! The last one was met with a chorus of laughter and refocus! The group had re-energized, feeling my enthusiasm. Everyone around me was huffing and puffing, but still running towards the finish.

Mile 23 was upon us and the group was feeling every muscle in their bodies. I needed a new distraction. I told the remaining three or four runners in our group to focus on a point ahead (a tree, a building, etc) and imagine that we would get there soon. Instead of seeing a giant 3.2 miles ahead, I wanted them to focus on a series of small, attainable goals.

At Mile 25 Cathy was hurting a lot. I offered her my hand and said, "You got this!." She held my hand until we saw the finish line. I had to keep my pace time of 5:00 but Cathy had a chance to finish with a faster time. She let go of my hand and ran with all her might across the finish line. She thanked me and said that I made her impossible mission possible.

She is my dear friend to this day and she still goes through the ABC's when she exercises and finds herself in need of a little extra push. She invited me to be her guest if I ran in Oklahoma.

Cathy gave me this shirt and cape ensemble I wore to work for "Super Hero Day" at my school.

2010: (30 marathons)

4/25/2010 Oklahoma City Memorial Marathon, Oklahoma

I stayed with my friend Cathy Ozeroglu. On Saturday morning, she arranged for me to have a massage, which was heavenly! I was pacing 4:30 and crossed at 4:29:49-can't get much closer than that!

5/29/2010 Bayshore Marathon, Michigan

I returned to Traverse City to pace my dear friend, Gayle McMurry, who not only wanted to re-qualify for Boston, but also wanted to break 4 hours. I stayed at a hotel near the race start the night before the marathon. The day of the marathon was warm and sunny. Gayle began to fade about the halfway point as the heat and humidity started to take its toll. Gayle's husband, Mike, met us along the course and ran with us to offer support. We finished in a time of 4:09:15. She did not meet her original time goal, but she re-qualified for Boston, and reached a PR at the same time!!

Me and Gayle McMurray

7/18/2010 Rio de Janeiro Marathan, Brazil

When I had met the race director for the Rio marathon in New York City, he invited me to run it. The day before, he gave me tickets for the pasta dinner. My roommates, Eileen and Diana, and I attended the dinner and it was an absolute smorgasbord! Each side room had a theme: pasta in one room, pizza in another room, and even steaks! The salad bar appeared to go on for miles and the desserts were decadent.

The race began as normal, but at Mile 21, I realized we were off course! I instructed Diana to stay put and I went ahead to scope things out. My suspicions were confirmed. We were off course. Apparently, a group of skaters and skateboarders had blocked our line of sight and we didn't see the directional cone, so we missed the turn. We saw one other runner up ahead and I told him that we were off course and needed to turn around. After adding a two mile detour, we found our way back to the pylons. Diana told me to go ahead and finish the race. I finished the race and told the volunteers that Diana was five miles behind me. Since the race had already closed, I accepted her medal on her behalf, just like the Oscars. Worried about my friend, I decided to check the medical tent where I saw Diana on a cot. Sick, but okay and very happy to accept her medal!

The next day, a bunch of people from the race took a cable car to Mount Corcovado in the Sugarloaf Mountains to see the statute of Christ the Redeemer. It was extraordinary. Next we went to the Copacabana Beaches and saw a lot of people playing soccer in the sand. I made sure to pick up a Brazil shirt for my nephew, Alex.

The next day, I got a tour guide to drive me up the mountain for my first hang-gliding experience. At the top of the mountain, we took ten steps and then we were off. After a breathtaking five minute ride, we landed on the beach.

7/25/2010 Ironman Triathlon Lake Placid, New York

Kayla was a student I taught from first through fifth grade. She had been battling cancer for several years. Now that she was 11

Lake Placid Triathlon volunteer and me

years old, I would be dedicating Mile 11 to her. I wore her picture on the back of my shirt.

During the swimming portion of the race, the rain was coming down hard, churning the lake. Lake Placid wasn't so placid after all! Thankfully, Lake Placid had a sightline at the bottom from the past Olympic games. The line made it so much easier. With a bunch of people starting with me, it was like a whirlpool. The crowd was spinning like socks in a washing machine. At the start, I got hit in the face by someone and lost my goggles. I was scared, so I went off to the side where there were fewer people. I put my goggles back on and tried to relax so that I could finish the race. I ended up finishing in 1:36.

By the time I finished the swim there weren't many bikes left. I spotted my bike right away, and didn't have to fight through the crowd to get it. The rain was still coming down hard. The bike race started with a big down hill, and I was scared. Instead of gaining speed, I had my brakes on the whole time. A quarter of the way through the race, the rain stopped. I felt a sense of relief. Finally, I could make up some lost time. I picked up speed and passed a lot of people. I was feeling proud, until I saw colossal hills ahead. There were three of them. Goldilocks was on her bike and approached the small hill, Baby Bear. Next, Mama Bear hill, and then came Papa Bear hill. Thinking of these hills as fairytale characters made them less them less threatening. After the third hill, Goldilocks wasn't able to eat the porridge yet! It was time to do the course a second time.

Next came the running portion. Since I wasn't going for a win, the running portion didn't matter. It was a powerful run. It was an enlivening run.

8/01/2010 Burning River 100 mile Endurance Race, Cuyahoga, Ohio

This is a 100 mile race, not even a full week after the Ironman in Lake Placid. In addition to being a challenging course, this is also the closest 100 mile race to Pittsburgh. I completed it in 25:44:10. I enjoy this race so much that I've run it a total of eight times, so far. I was the first place runner in my age group three times!

I had two pacers for this race. The rule is competitors can have pacers only between miles 53 and 100. My two pacers were my boyfriend, John, who took miles 53-76, and Marty Butler, who paced me from 76 to 100. It was raining, and REALLY muddy.

Burning River Buckle

I saw a lot of runners slip, fall, and face-plant and almost shared their fate several times. Actually, I did slip and fall once but I sprang right back up (no face-plant!). This wound up being my second slowest finish, second only to 2014, when I had been in a car accident the day before the race!

8/21/2010 Reykjavik Marathon, Reykjavik City, Iceland

I had travelled to Iceland with Marathon Tours. I wanted to sight-see as much as possible because I didn't know if I would ever have the chance to go to Iceland again. I got to see Reykjavik and the lava field. The Blue Lagoon geothermal spa was fantastic! I had a roommate named Roy. We went on a horseback ride. For the record, I did not step on Roy's shoes. His horse stepped on them!

However, no amount of Icelandic beauty could take away the pain of losing my friend, Kayla. Just two days before the race, I got news from Kayla's mom that Kayla had died on August 19. I was devastated. I decided I would dedicate this race to her. It crushed my spirits, and I didn't want to come home.

I dedicated Mile 11 in Kayla's memory.

Kayla Rush and me

Kayla's family and me,. Berenato's Bunch

Kayla Rush and me

11/7/2010 New York City Marathon, New York

I found out that I was pacing a man named Elton on the day of the race. In Berlin, Elton was the equivalent to our Jay Leno. Elton had placed a bet whether or not he could complete a marathon. I became his exclusive pacer for the race. The pressure was on, but I knew I could do it! Spectators recognized him along the way and were chanting his name. He finished the race with me in 5:00, our original pace time and hugged me! Elton was so impressed that he wanted me to run the Berlin, Marathon, but I was not able to that year. I did eventually run in the Berlin Marathon.

11/21/2010 Philadelphia Marathon, Pennsylvania

I met and paced Tina Brinkerhoff of Philadelphia. I was pacing 5:30 and came in at 5:29:19. Tina had leg pain and was sick. She wanted to stay by me the whole time. We kept in touch after the race and became good friends.

2011: (26 marathons)

2/06/2011 Surf City USA Marathan, Huntington, California

I was scheduled to pace 4:30. I had no place to stay, but the pace leader put me in touch with Rob and Sue Zihlmenn. Sue, born in South Africa had a wall of medals, many of them 1st place awards.

2/20/2011 Shamrock Sports Fest Marathon, Virginia Beach, Virginia

It was my 200th marathon. Tina drove from Philadelphia. The night before the race, we had dinner and she brought out a cake with candles to celebrate my 200th marathon.

5/08/11 Kalamazoo Marathon, Michigan

Traveling from Atlanta and Philadelphia, my friends and fellow runners, Eileen and Tina, met me at my Mom's house, along with my brother, Tom, from South Bend. Tom surprised me by bringing a special guest to the finish line. I cried tears of joy as my mom reached out to place the medal around my neck. I was pacing at 4:45 and finished the race at 4:44:15.

5/15/11 Pittsburgh Marathon, Pennsylvania

I was awarded the Pheidippides Award in recognition of the endurance, victory, and triumph of the human spirit. The award was presented by the directors of the Pittsburgh Marathan.

5/29/2011 Vermont City Marathon, Burltington, Vermont

People may think that the most difficult part of a race would be the actual marathon or half marathon, but it's not. The travel situation for this race was terrible. I was to fly by myself from Pittsburgh to Philadelphia and then Philadelphia to Vermont. I boarded the plane to Vermont (supposedly). I fell asleep and woke to hear the pilot announce there was no visibility at all. We were near the airport, but our descent was thwarted by the weather. We were on our way to Manchester, New Hampshire. I DIDN'T WANT TO GO TO NEW HAMPSHIRE! From the groans aboard the plane, I figured the other passengers didn't want to go there either!

Welcome to New Hampshire. My first stop was at the ticket counter where I was third in line (Hurray!), but the representative explained that I would need to stay overnight in a hotel, fly back to Philadelphia and take a plane to Vermont. That was not a good plan AT ALL! Plan "B" was to rent a car and drive a few hours from New Hampshire to Vermont. This was a much more palatable option until I found a line at the rental counter as long as the checkout lines at Walmart on Black Friday. I was next in line. The agent announced that the customer in front of me had gotten the last car! I cried! At least the hotel room was comped. Back at the hotel, I had to devise a Plan "C" so I called Tina in Philadelphia. Tina offered to drive to New Hampshire, pick me up, and drive to Vermont. The next day, Tina ended up driving three people to Vermont. We had met on the plane and we were all headed to the marathon. Tina and I ran the marathon together. I paced 4:45 and came in at 4:44:20. We both stayed at Margaret Ferguson's house that night. We met through my demonstrator position at House of Lloyd's. A store, "Ski Rack," gave me Mizuno shoes and shorts for the race. The rest of the weekend was uneventful, but you can see how traveling can be a roller coaster ride. The New Hampshire detour was just one of many that I encountered in my travels, but from having to deplane because of a bird in the propeller, to mechanical difficulties, and assorted weather-related delays. These delays are annoying at the time, God has always looked out for me as I travel.

9/11/2011 Rev 3 Cedar Point Ironman Triathlon, Sandunsky, Ohio

The 2.4 mile swim was great! I brought my own bike and anchored an American flag on the back to honor the memory of those lost on September 11, 2001. I was having a good day until the second loop biking. I cut my finger bad! when I hit a sign. When another rider cut me off, I biked into the sign. John came out riding the bike course backwards looking for me. He found me with blood all over my bike. "What happened?" he asked. "I hit a sign," I replied. He rode ahead to the transition area to tell them that I was coming in with a bad cut. He told them that I would not stop if they tried

Rev 3 Triathlon Bike start

Rev 3 Triathlon Medal.

to remove me. He was right! John told them to just bandage me up enough to allow me to finish. So they bandaged me and I continued. My sister, Anne, and my niece, Olivia, were there at Mile Marker 1. I waved and blew them a kiss. So, at the end of the race, #431, Marie Bartoletti finished an Ironman.

I went over to the medical tent to have my finger looked at and they gave me an IV (standard procedure). As I was getting my IV, I was cold so they gave me a blanket and I covered up my head, even though John told me not to because I looked like a dead body. Now came the time for stitches. I was given a shot to numb the area. After two shots, I could still feel it. As the doctor started to stitch me, I was screaming. So, the doctor gave me another shot and began to stitch again. The area still was not numb but he continued. I screamed with every prick of the needle. I asked, "How many more stitches?" He told me that there were two more stitches to go. I replied, "You are done!" I wouldn't let him continue.

My niece, Olivia, and nephew, Sam, and my boyfriend, John

Before the ride, I had spent some time with my niece, nephew and sister as well as my boyfriend John.

After the race, John went thru a red light, and the Sandusky police pulled us over. He just gave us a warning and told us to be careful. He knew that I just did an Ironman, because my bike was on the back of the car.

11/20/2011 Route 66 Marathon, Tulsa, Oklahoma

I paced the race and Diana Burton wanted to go with me. She didn't say why. We started together. Twenty miles, five hours in the race, she said "Goodbye." She hugged me and I didn't know why. I finished at 5:29:03 as a 5:30 pacer. The day, and Diana's run, became even more curious when she asked me for my mailing address after the race. A week later, I got a Peacock Sparkle Skirt in the mail from Diana. That made me feel good and appreciated. Her elusive behavior became clearer when she confided in me that she was gearing up for her 100th marathon in Stockholm, Sweden.

A requirement for Stockholm is that runners must reach a specific bridge in 5 hours. I had registered for the Stockholm Marathon earlier that month, as did Tina, John and now, Diana.

2012: (22 marathons)

4/08/2012 Comrades Ultramarathon, Durbin, South Africa

"The Ultimate Human Race" is the world's largest and oldest ultramarathon. I left Pittsburgh and landed in Detroit expecting to connect with a plane for South Africa. I was furious and uncertain of how I was going to get to South Africa. I spoke with the agent at the service desk and she found a way for me to get there. It took an additional two planes and an extra half day of travel. It was Easter weekend and I had a few extra days off from my teaching job. The race was 56 miles (90 km). More than 60 countries were represented among the 20,000 runners.

Comrades Medal

I wore a USA shirt and many commented on it along the course, making me proud. My race number was 30230 and my finish time was 10:12:11. My travel plans altered and I wasn't able to stay for an African safari. I wanted to see some of the beauty that Africa had to offer. So, after completing the ultramarathon, I walked alone to the aquarium where I volunteered (and was chosen!) to feed the dolphins during the show. They are so graceful and docile and one of my favorites.

7/2012 Stockholm Marathon, Sweden

Tina, Diana, John, and I went several days early to acclimate to the time difference, get some pre-marathon training in, and take in the sights. This was the 100th anniversary of the Stockholm Olympics. People were dressed as they would have been 100 years ago. At the Expo, there were classic/antique cars, fire trucks, and bicycles. It was quite a sight to behold. The reproduction felt like the real thing. A fireman himself, John was especially impressed with the antique fire trucks. I took a picture of him with one. Because I do not speak Swedish, I could not be an official pacer. On my way out of the hotel the morning of the race, I got a balloon and wrote in pen, "Diana's 100th marathon." As I got to the starting line, a bunch of people signed the balloon. I held the balloon as I ran. I ran in the skirt that Diana gave me. About 5 miles in, we saw the "official" pacer with two people in his group. I took a quick look around me and realized my balloon and I had about seven people in my "unofficial" pacing group. Another quick glance at Mile 10, and my group had flourished to 10 runners. As I looked around, I kept seeing the same hat in the crowd. I wanted that hat. So at Mile 14, a race coordinator gave me his hat. At Mile 17, there were about 13 runners with me. Apparently my hat, balloon, and singing were drawing a crowd. Yes, I sing when I run. Then I realized I had backup singers with the group singing along. We had the option the do 40K (that was the distance run in 1912) or 42K (the recognized distance today). We opted to do 42K!

John, Tina, and I got a flight to Demark. John and I took a tour of a church. We spiraled up the steeple and reached a point where we had to back down or go outside the steeple and continue spiraling up the outside. As we were heading up the outside, the steps were getting narrower and narrower. Finally, at the top step there was only room for one of your feet. I was scared to go up, afraid of heights! Backwards to get down! I conquered it! The end of the day we went to "Ice Bar." This was invigorating. The bar was "cool" in more ways than one. Everything from the walls to the drinking glasses were made of ice! They gave us robes that went all the way to the floor to keep us warm. That was the "COOLEST" bar I have been to.

The next day John, Mike G, and I rode bicycles from the hotel. Mine had a ringer bell and a basket like the Wicked Witch's bike from the Wizard of Oz! State of the art, the bike had one speed! We rode 70K, start stopping at the oldest amusement park in Europe. Mike G and I hopped on the roller coaster. We biked a little farther and Mike G and John stopped to eat, but I didn't. I continued to the Castle. I got to the Castle about half an hour before it closed. Mike and John got there 5 minutes after it closed. We rode back in a hurry. The next day we stopped at the Vassar Museum, which was awesome. It was neat seeing the ship that capsized on its maiden voyage.

8/11/2012 New York City Ironman Triathlon, New York

Two days before the event, there was a sewage spill on the Hudson River. Officials debated whether to allow the swim. The bacteria count in the water dropped and we were okay. My friend, Tina Brinkerhoff, John, and I shared a hotel room. John was not racing, but Tina and I were attempting to get a best personal. Before the race, they take a highlighter marker and write each participant's age prominently on one leg and arm. During the race, I could track others in my age group to monitor how I was doing. My swim was very fast. Halfway through I thought my watch had stopped! I got out of the water at an hour and 5 minutes, having shaved off half an hour from my previous best swim.

Five miles into the bike ride I heard a fellow say, "Nice legs!." That woke me up! I followed him for 20 miles. I had seen a spectator with a Lady Liberty hat and said, "Nice hat!." The route was a 65 mile loop, so on my second pass through, I saw the same spectator and said, "I want your hat." I saw him once more, and he held out his hat for me to take! I stopped and got off my bike and thanked him for the hat. When the run started, I swapped my bike helmet for the Lady Liberty hat! I was high fiving everyone and having fun. My finish time may have been a little better had Lady Liberty not blown off my head! I went back to retrieve the hat! The runners climbed stairs to the bridge, yes, stairs in an Ironman! My fear of heights struck, causing me to vomit. After that brief pause, I was back running. I high fived a volunteer and told her, "I love the volunteers!" Little did I know that a cameraman happened to be nearby. The video clip made it to the New York City Ironman Triathalon highlights! I saw John and he told me I was in 4th place; two minutes back. I told him that I was tired and didn't care. He told me to do what I want, gave me a disgusted look and walked away. Then, I started thinking Kona. Kona was within my reach! As I was running with renewed energy, I kept looking for body markings on everyone's calves. Then I found and passed her! She had a Marmaduke dog on her trisuit at 22 miles. There was a group of spectators with the same shirts. They started cheering as I passed them and she was right behind me. I kept pushing. I didn't want her to pass me. Then, I saw the finish line! I had done it. At this point, I was in pretty rough shape. I should have gone to medical but I wanted to find John. We found each other in the finish area and his first words to me were, "Congratulations, you should be in medical." I told him I was ok and just needed to sit down. We found a wall to sit on where I passed out. John had to carry me 200 yards to the medical tent through a crowd of spectators at the finish line. He left all of our belongings on the wall; cell phone, money, wallet, everything! He asked the woman who was sitting beside us to bring it to the medical tent. Luckily, she was an honest person, and we got everything back. After spending a few hours in the medical tent receiving IVs and hydration, I was released in time to see my friend, Tina, complete her first IM! Success all around! I immediately signed up for Kona, "The World Championship!"

8/13/2012 Monday after the Ironman. I was scheduled for surgery. In July, I had been diagnosed with a treatable form of cancer. The surgery was an outpatient procedure but my recovery time was supposed to be 2 weeks. I was worried, not only because of the cancer diagnosis, but KONA was coming up and I needed to be in top shape. All of the hotels in the area were booked, but John found a house to rent. The owner's mother even picked us up at the airport and drove us to pick up my rental bike for the race (more about that later)!

9/21/2012 It was three weeks before Kona. It was around 5:30 in the evening. I had coached tennis and was trying to get in a ride for Kona training. Disaster struck. That afternoon biking through a popular County Park, I hit a telephone pole. To this day, I have no idea how. When I regained consciousness, I was in the hospital alone. It took a long time to piece all of the details together. I was told the paramedics and police responded quickly, but they didn't know who I was. (Lesson learned. From that day forward, I always carried ID). One of the Good Samaritans on the scene, Jessica Navoney, the aquatics director at Healthtrax, recognized me and gave my name to the first responders. The doctors told me that I had a concussion, even though I had been wearing a helmet. I remained in the hospital overnight and was released the next day. I explained to the doctor that I was going to compete at Kona and he said I was cleared to compete, but advised me to stop if my concussion symptoms returned. I went to work the next day. My first grade students were the first to show concern. They asked, "What happened to your eye?" I had a black eye. They were so nice to be concerned.

9/25/2012 Quad Cities Marathon, Moline, Illinois

This marathon spans Illinois and Iowa, with the Mississippi River running in between. All participants were given gloves and each finger represented a "big" city in the Quad Cities: Rock Island, Moline, East Moline in Illinois, Davenport and Bettendorf in Iowa. I was scheduled to pace the 4:55 group. I arrived at the marathon still sporting a black eye from my bike accident four days before. I told the pace leader that I had a concussion and I would have to stop if the symptoms returned. Fortunately, all went well and I came in at 4:54:56. Four seconds under, but who's counting?

10/11/2012 World Championship Ironman, Kona, Hawaii

The doctor told me it was ok to compete but I had to stop if I had concussion symptoms from my bike accident three weeks before. According to the race rules, if I didn't compete, I had to re-qualify the following year.

We had rented a house from Gus and his mother, Vivian, picked John and me up at the airport and she took me to the bike rental shop. From there, she drove John to Gus's house. I chose to bike there. Little did I know that the house was high on a hill. Every day, I would wake and cycle 5 miles from the house to the morning swim. It was not easy. I would pray during the swim. At

Ironman Kona Medal

the turnaround of the morning swim, there was a coffee barge in the water, "Free KONA Coffee!" I would stop. I asked the workers if they would be back the following day, but they said they wouldn't be because of the World Championship race. They got a kick out of me asking.

H POST-GAZETTE ■ THURSDAY, NOVEMBER 15, 2012 ■ WWW.POST-GAZETTE.COM

RESUME: A newsmaker you should know

Phys ed teacher, triathlon veteran leads by example

By Rita Michel

Students at McClellan Elementary School in the West Jefferson Hills School District have to move fast to keep up with their physical education teacher: Marie Bartoletti, who has taught fitness to students there for 17 years, just completed another triathlon.

"It was tough," says the 55-year-old Bethel Park resident, about the Kona Ironman Championship that took place in Hawaii in mid-October. She was one of 1,800 athletes from across the world who qualified for the event.

First, Ms. Bartoletti swam 2.4 miles in "the biggest swells ever," she said.

Volunteers who patrolled the event from kayaks to keep the competitors safe, provided encouragement, she said. "They told me it would be easier going back because the waves were so big."

She didn't get to dry off during the 112-mile biking portion of the event that followed, because of drenching rains and wicked crosswinds.

"I was a little bit nervous," said the veteran of several triathlons. "Every year it's windy but this year's was the windiest."

The final event, a 26.2-mile marathon, was just another fun run to the woman who runs about 30 marathons a year (sometimes two in one weekend) and volunteers as a pacer at marathons across the country, helping the other runners to make it across the finish line with encouragement and humor. She's a regular volunteer pacer at the Dick's Sporting Goods Pittsburgh Marathon, where she can be seen wearing one of her vast collection of funny hats.

She had a hat for the Hawaii event, too. It was created by an art teacher at McClelland and featured the Pittsburgh Marathon and next year's date, May 5, 2013.

Back at school after the Ironman event, Ms. Bartoletti quickly went to work getting her students ready to compete in the Punt, Pass and Kick competition at McClellan. Lily Rockwell, a fourth-grader, went on to the sectionals Oct. 21, where she won in both the girls' and the boys' 8- to 9-year-old division. Lily will attend the Dec. 9 Steelers-San Diego game at Heinz Field and participate in a punt, pass and kick event before the game.

Ms. Bartoletti has had students who make it to the finals in each of the 16 years she's trained students for the competition.

But just because that competition is over doesn't mean the McClellan students can rest. Their gym teacher is now getting them ready to run in the Kids of Steel race that takes place every year the day before the Pittsburgh Marathon. "We run a half-mile once a week here to get them in shape for running a mile," Ms. Bartoletti said.

The official Kids of Steel training program will begin Jan. 7 and continue for 16 weeks until this year's children's race, which takes place May 4. To qualify, the students must run 24 miles during the training program, completing the 25th mile at the event

tion. The boys' and girls' junior varsity tennis teams finished the season with only one loss.

Ms. Bartoletti, who grew up in Kalamazoo, Mich., was a nationally ranked tennis player while in college at Central Michigan University. When she first came to Pittsburgh, she played on the U.S. Tennis Association team in Mt. Lebanon. Her second year there, the team won the national competition in Palm Springs.

"I love all sports," Ms. Bartoletti said. "I think I got my athletic ability from my dad but my commitment to community service from my mom. Her first endeavor locally was introducing the National Heart Association's Jump Rope for the Heart competition to her elementary students. "My mom always said, 'It's nice to be important but more important to be nice.' "

And that's what led her from running marathons to pacing them. "I don't really care about winning races anymore," said the mother of two grown sons. "I've been there a few times."

SNAPSHOT

MARIE BARTOLETTI

AGE: 55

HOMETOWN: Bethel Park

OCCUPATION: Physical education teacher at McClellan Elementary and coach for junior varsity tennis at Thomas Jefferson High School, both in West Jefferson Hills School District

FAMILY: Sons, David, 28, who lives in Maine; and Michael, 27, who lives in Florida

EDUCATION: Bachelor's degree, Central Michigan University; national board certification in teaching

WHAT'S IMPORTANT TO YOU: "My kids and giving 100 percent all the time."

FIRST JOB: Baby-sitting; first paid job in Pittsburgh, taught K-12 physical education at Sacred Heart in East Liberty

AND WHEN YOU WERE A KID, YOU WANTED TO BE: "A teacher, like my dad."

HOBBIES: "I love to bake. ... I bring cookies to every faculty meeting."

READING MATERIAL: Janet Evanovich novels

WHAT'S ON YOUR TV: "Don't have one."

WHAT'S PLAYING ON YOUR IPOD: "Do not have one of these either, but like to listen to music on my MP3 player."

WHO WOULD PLAY YOU IN A MOVIE: "I have no idea. I don't go to the movies much."

GUILTY PLEASURE: Chocolate

DO OVER: "I would do everything the same way. I'm happy with my life the way it is. I feel very blessed."

FAVORITE SPOT: The beach. "I love all water sports."

PROUDEST MOMENT: "Besides delivering my two kids, when I was on the cover of the Wheaties box in 2003."

GOALS: Bike across America and back. "Not race, just ride."

BUCKET LIST: Ditto.

Kona Ironman article

10/13/2012 I woke up around 4:00 on the morning of the race. I had a quick bagel, a banana, and Gatorade and was on my way. Reality hit when I gave John a hug and kiss goodbye knowing that I would spend the next 14 to 18 hours pushing my body to its limits. I stood in line at the registration area with the other participants. Nervous does not begin to describe the feelings that I had. Remember being a child and waiting in line for the tallest roller coaster in the amusement park? That's how I felt.

Prior to triathlons, participants not only get a bib, but they also get their number drawn on an arm and a leg with permanent marker. Having been through this in New York, I was mentally prepared, but as I approached the volunteers at the check-in I saw that they were using stamps, not just permanent marker. It became very real and very scary. I cried tears of joy!

The first leg was swimming and the start was about 5 minutes from the check-in point. They were starting elites and I was impressed with their athleticism. Then I started. On the days leading up to the Ironman, the ocean was calm, but the morning of the event, the ocean was angry with large three foot swells. I was afraid I would not be able to make the swim. An hour and 15 minutes into it, I asked the volunteers in boats, "How far is it to the finish line?" I had serious doubts, but I did in it 1:59:19. At the end of the swimming leg, volunteers helped me out of the water.

Forty miles into the bike ride, it started to pour rain. I didn't want to pass, or be passed, by anyone. I was shaking. It was a hill. Then I got to the run. At the start, I felt fine. But at Mile 16, I started to get nauseous and had to alternate between walking and running, using the orange cones that lined the race route to cue me to switch. By then, it was dark, and my frustration had reached its peak.

I kept moving forward. I eventually found the finish line! It was great to hear, "Marie Bartoletti, you are an IRONMAN!" I completed it in 14:50:27, not the best time, but an Ironman Finisher! It was as good as I could do under the circumstances.

2013: (23 marathons)

2/03/2013 Surf City USA Marathon, Huntington, California

I had paced 4:40 and came in at 4:39:20. After the race, I was busy collecting beer tickets from the runners. Then I went into the "beer tent" to start drinking. I was having a blast! When the security guard approached John he asked, "Is she with you?" Apparently I was having TOO much fun! They asked me to leave the tent. I left the beer tent and the security guard told John, "She can't be here! She has to leave the premises." I had to stand on the sidewalk, public property! It was the equivalent of a "Beer Tent Time Out!" I was staying at Maneesha's house. She was one of the women I ran Badwater with. It happened that it was also Super Bowl Sunday, so we returned to Maneesha's house to watch the game together.

8/25/2013 IRONMAN Louisville, Kentucky

John and I stayed with Bill and Kelly Stearman, whom I met through a local running store, Fleet Feet. (The following year, I got Bill to run an Ironman with me.) Everyone was getting in a line to jump in the water as pairs. I went in with Bill. I got fourth place in my division at 13:21:42! I dropped almost 2 hours from my previous Ironman in Mt. Tremblant, partly because this course was flatter, the weather was milder, and I had prepared my body better.

2014: (27 marathons)

8/17/2014 Ironman Mont-Tremblant, Quebec, Canada

John and I stopped at Beniot's house in Hudson, Quebec. Benoit spoke English and French. I ran with his girlfriend, Mimi. Beniot's mother, Francine, took us out to dinner. The next day, we got to Mont-Tremblant. It is most spectacular place to host an Ironman. It is a resort! We took a gondola to the top of the mountain. The weather was foggy so we didn't see much. The dinner was absolutely amazing. They had performers, trapeze artists, and trampolines. The next day was the Ironman. The water was a cold, 65 degrees for the swim. I swam, and I was shaking. I had to wear a wet trisuit. My head was cold even with a hat under my helmet. The first downhill was terrible. I was shaking from my head to my feet. I got dry clothes from a spectator. Medical checked me and I refused treatment. I was supposed to stop at the next aid station. I blew right past them and waved. I had only 20 minutes left before being cut-off for the run. I was running fast the first half of the run. The second half, I was weak and sick. I finished the race. I was taken out to the medical tent where I was given an IV and anti-nausea drug. I continued to vomit. My time was 15:20:14. I was lucky I finished. The next day I was not feeling too good, but was grateful to have heard the words, "Marie Bartoletti, you are an Ironman!"

Mont-Tremblant Ironman Expo with John

2015: (26 marathons)

11/01/2015 New York City Marathon

The pace team leader asked if I would pace an individual one on one. I agreed but was not told who it was. When we met that day, learned she was a sports agent for Maria Sharapova (pro tennis player) and Cam Newton (pro football player). This chance meeting, upon later reflection, had a larger meaning for me. She was a stroke survivor, and her husband was running with her. She invited me into the VIP tent. She stood by me, but I remained rather quiet because I technically wasn't supposed to be there. Throughout the race, people were chanting her name and cheering her on. Her husband started to get sore so I offered him an Aleve. As a pacer, I have a feeling of responsibility. I feel it is my duty to keep my runners going no matter what. And I did my job, bringing her in at 6:04. She was happy and I was happy for her!

2/15/2015 Ft Lauderdale A1A Marathon, Florida

This would be my 300th marathon and I was pacing 4:40.My friend, Tina, lives in Florida and made the two hour drive over

28 • FEBRUARY 05, 2015 • SOUTH HILLS RECORD

WJH phys ed teacher completes 300th marathon

BY JENNIFER GOGA

Marie Bartoletti's friends and fellow runners call her the "Energizer bunny" because she exhibits the same endless energy of the marketing mascot for Energizer batteries.

LOCAL SCENE

Earlier this month, Bartolettti, 57, of Bethel Park, completed her 300th marathon in Ft. Lauderdale, Fla.

After running her first marathon in 1994, she soon discovered a love for "pacing" marathons. Since 2004, Bartoletti has averaged 25 to 30 marathons and has run a marathon in every state in America.

"Pacing is my passion," she said. "It makes me feel good to help other runners qualify for the Boston Marathon or get their personal best."

In her role as a marathon pacer, Bartoletti carries a long stick with balloons and a time on it as she runs. She maintains that pace throughout the race.

Anyone who wants to finish the race at that pace runs alongside Bartoletti for the duration of the race.

"As a pacer, I set a speed for the race," Bartoletti said.

Recently, Bartoletti has been running at the 4:45 pace, which is about 10.5 minutes per mile. Her own personal-best time for a marathon was 3:40, set 10 years ago. More recently, she registered a 3:59 time.

But since she paces the race at a slower pace, it allows her to encourage the runners around her and keep them motivated.

"I'm basically a cheerleader. I try to make it fun. I sing and tell stories as we're running," Baroletti said "People call me 'Pacer Marie,' and now they look for me at races from year to year."

Bartoletti often gets e-mails from runners she has paced, thanking her for getting them through their marathon.

She keeps busy during the week, teaching physical education at McClellan Elementary School in the West Jefferson Hills School District, where she started a running club for students in conjunction with the Pittsburgh Marathon.

She also is an assistant coach for the Thomas Jefferson High School boys' and girls' tennis teams.

After 10 years, Bartoletti has a pretty consistent marathon schedule that takes her all over the country on just about every other weekend. She finished marathons in every state over the course of two years, from 2004 to 2005.

"I don't spend money on anything else, and I usually stay with friends in each city," Bartoletti said. "I just love it."

Her 300th marathon was memorable for other reasons besides reaching the impressive milestone.

Bartoletti came down with a virus just before the race, but managed to power her way to the finish line despite not feeling well.

"I was not my usual 'Energizer bunny' self," she said. "I just kept drinking water and Gatorade."

Even after completing 300 marathons, Bartoletti doesn't plan to slow down or stop pacing marathons anytime soon.

"As long as I feel good, I'm going to keep doing it," she said. "It gives me a good feeling to help other runners."

Jennifer Goga is a freelance writer.

SUBMITTED PHOTO

Marie Bartoletti, a physical education teacher at McClellan Elementary School, is a "pacer" for marathons across the country. Since 2004, Bartoletti has averaged 25 to 30 marathons per year, and has run a marathon in every state. In her role as pacer, she carries a long stick with balloons and a time on it.

300th Marathon article

to the race to surprise me! I was staying with my friend, Marcela, who is also friends with Tina, so we spent time catching up with each other. I was assigned a race number, but my results were not posted to the marathon results website. It still counted as my 300th marathon, phew! One of my local newspapers printed a story about my accomplishment. I was beyond proud! My friend, Diana Burton, had a bobblehead trophy made in honor of my 300th marathon.

4/19/2015 Athens Ohio Marathon

I was especially excited for this marathon because it was the first marathon for Gabriel, Elizabeth, Belle, and Steve Snyder. Gabriel, Elizabeth, and Belle were students of mine and had trained to run this marathon. We ran as a group, cheering each other on along the way and finished at 5:43!

Snyder Children's first marathon

2016: (30 marathons)

2/14/2016 Ft. Lauderdale A1A Marathon, Florida

I was pacing 4:30. John and I were staying with Marcela. I got sick! Not just ordinary sick, I had the Norwalk virus. I couldn't eat anything. I suspected I picked up the virus from the plane. It hit me like a ton of bricks. The morning of the race, I still couldn't eat but I managed to get a banana in. The whole race, I didn't feel well at all, but I hit my time 4:29:50. I got into the medical tent and was immediately transferred to the hospital. Three hours later, I was released from the hospital. It was nice to be surrounded by John, Marcela and her husband.

3/06/2016 Little Rock Marathon, Arkansas' Race for Every Pace

I was pacing 4:40 and came in at 4:38:50. John was pacing 4:30, so he was scheduled to come in 10 minutes before me. This was my 5th marathon after my stroke, I was so proud to resume pacing along with Gina and Geneva, the "CIC". John was faithfully waiting for me at the finish line. As I was finishing, an announcement was made that this was my 325th marathon and that number 320 should have been my last. As I finished, there was a television crew waiting to do an interview. The finish line is sometimes a conglomeration of people and activity. John usually tries to get me to drink something and I usually want to find everyone from my pacing group. Now there was an interviewer in the mix. John had already informed the reporter that I was having a difficult time with my speech following my stroke. When the reporter got to me, all I could say was, "I love pacing." Had it not been for the stroke, I would have been talking up a storm with the reporter. But as it was, I was just glad to be able to tell about my love of pacing. As the interview was happening, I saw Richard. He is a wheelchair participant that I see in Little Rock every year. I ran over to him, and we hugged each other, both proud of our accomplishments. John finished the interview by telling the reporter, that I was mentally the toughest person he knew. We did not see the newscast that evening, but we did see it as we were getting ready to leave the hotel Monday morning. It was kind of strange to see yourself on the television in the morning.

5/15/2016 Cleveland Marathon, Ohio

Saturday morning, I arrived at Steve's house. I had taught his three children and had run with them in the past. We drove to Cleveland together, and I thoroughly enjoyed the conversations in the car. It was a unique experience traveling with a young family versus traveling by myself. We ran the race together and the kids were elated to get their medals!

Snyders at Cleveland Marathon

9/25/2016 Berlin Marathon, Germany

I was traveling overseas by myself and was scared. I didn't speak German, and since my stroke, it was even difficult to speak in my native language. My first hurdle was to book my flight. When speaking with the airline agent, I first explained my

Berlin Marathon.

situation. In my post-stroke, halting manner, I told the agent, "I had a stroke. Please be patient with me." She was very patient as I made my arrangements. It was official, I was on my way to Germany! The marathon tour group assigned me a roommate, Thanh Clark. She and I hit it off right away. We ran a 5K on Saturday, and watched a roller skating marathon together. That was a first for me. I'd never seen a marathon on roller skates. I toured the beautiful town and took in all of the sights. All of my fears subsided. I was able to enjoy all that Germany had to offer.

11/06/2016 New York City Marathon

I stayed with my friend, Tina, who was also registered to run. Tina had recently moved from Philadelphia to NYC. We took the ferry over to the starting area. It was the first time I had taken a ferry. It was a powerful experience and pumped me up for the race. I felt alive! I was pacing 4:40 and crossed at 4:39:25. Another delightful marathon experience in NYC!

12/31/2016 and 1/01/2017 New Year's Double, Dallas, Texas

This is a "double" which means we run two days in a row. I won BOTH races (4:45 and 4:45)! What better way to celebrate the win than double fisting some well-deserved refreshments.

1/29/2017 Miami Marathon, Florida

This was my 15th year pacing this marathon. Marcela was also running the Miami Marathon for the 15th year. She picked me up from my flight, and we went to a party that the race director was having for everyone who had run the race for 15 years. I was pacing the race at 4:40 and came in at 4:39:11. There were a whole bunch of people with me while I was pacing.

2/04/2017 Groundhog Marathon Grand Rapids, Michigan

I enjoy wearing costumes and hats when I run. But this particular marathon had a special meaning. Donna, my speech therapist, did a fabulous job, a custom crocheted groundhog outfit. I won first place for my age in the costume contest!

Near Year's Double, Dollas, Texas

Marcela Todd and me

Groundhog Day Marathon

3/05/2017 Little Rock Marathon, Arkansas' Race for Every Pace

The theme this year was "Runalicious." I dressed as a Starlight peppermint candy. My cellophane wrapper rustled for the entire race. The crinkling of the wrapper caused me to flash back to the days of my youth, sitting in a church on Sunday, unwrapping a butter scotch candy during the quiestest part of Mass within earshot of a parishioner. I came in at 4:39 with a smile on my face knowing that the runners behind me were consumed with my 26.2 mile of crinkles!

Little Rock Marathon Candy Theme

3/12/2017-Barcelona Marathon, Spain

At the Chicago, Marathon, I was picked out to pace the Barcelona Marathon. I was the only pacer who could speak English, and I was one of only two girls to pace for this race. I was one of three people pacing 4:30. One of the other pacers in my group had a problem with his shoes and had to leave the race after only 20 miles. The other pacer and I finished at 4:29:59. Barcelona, Spain was gorgeous!

Barcelona Marathon

Barcelona Marathon Pace Team

Barcelona Marathon

3/19/2017 Publix Marathon, Atlanta, Georgia

My friend, Eileen, picked me up at the airport. I was staying with her. On Saturday morning, Eileen and I did three miles with a group of other marathon runners. We went to the Expo together, and Eileen saw lots of people that she knew. The next day, we got a train ride to the start line. During the race, two guys that Eileen knew were following me from the start line so that I could pace for them even though I wasn't officially a pacer for this race. The course was very hilly. I came in at 4:15 and received second place. Two weeks later, to my surprise, I got a mini Publix shopping cart sent to my house. That was the first time I had ever gotten a shopping cart as a trophy!

Mini Publix shopping cart trophy

4/02/2017 Rome Marathon, Italy

I booked my trip through Marathon Tours and traveled by myself. I went to the Colosseum, and I ran into a man I knew from Columbus, Ohio. The tour of Rome was fantastic! I decided to take a walking tour to Santa Maria Maggiore Basilica. I met the Pastor there and genuflected at the altar. It was a powerful experience I will never forget!

The following day at the Expo I was surprised to see Roman gladiators in costume, of course, making their rounds. I also met a gentleman, working at one of the booths, that I would end up pacing!

This was obviously a new course for me and I wanted to meet my 4:30 pacing time. Before the race, a man approached and hugged me. It's always great to see other people in a foreign country. This gentlemen was from Atlanta, Georgia. It was raining at the start of the race. The rain stopped for a bit midway through the race, but resumed later. The rain added a new dimension because the cobblestone road became slippery (or

Rome Marathon

as we say in Pittsburgh, "Slippy"). Fortunately, I didn't fall, but I saw at least 3 people go down. I crossed the finish line at 4:29:30.

4/22/2017 Carmel Marathon, Indiana

My cousin, Patty Warrick, awaited me at the Expo. I had paced this race nine times in the last nine years! Patty took me out to a restaurant for pizza. It was GREAT! I read her my "back story," and she was laughing. She gave me a letter I wrote to her family when I was growing up. It was hysterical I was so young.

The race director had been in Little Rock, Arkansas. I recognized him and we hugged. I hugged him and he hugged me! I was pacing this marathon at 4:40 Lots of people were doing my pace. It was different than last year. The hills were taken out—yeah! I came in with 4 people; it was SO NICE! 4:39:40. After I got out from the finish line, I took a bus to the hotel (it was paid for!). I had to hurry up and get a shower to go to the next marathon. I had to drive to Toledo, Ohio.

4/23/2017 Glass City Marathon, Toledo, Ohio

John met me at the Expo. Jim Poole, in charge of "Dave's Running Store," graciously paid for all the pacers' shoes and he got the "Dave's Running Store" pacers shirts. So Saturday night, John and I headed over to the store to pick up our gear. We went to the same mass we went to the previous four years. The priest said he was doing the half marathon. I wished him luck outside the church. Then we got to the Park Inn, which was paid for by the Toledo Marathon. I got up the next day, paced 4:45, and came in at 4:44:53. I recognized lot of people from the previous year.

6/3/2017 God's Country Marathon, Coudersport, Pennsylvania

John and I were going to race this, not pace! I stayed at John's hunting cabin, where I had my choice of about 10 sleeping bags. Next day, John's car didn't start! John said, "We have to walk to the start line or we can't do it." What do you think I said? We walked to the start line, five miles away. I got first place in my age division 4:16:13!

6/10/2017 Hatfield McCoy Marathon, Williamson, West Virginia and Kentucky

I drove by myself. Friday, I got to the Expo. I was pacing and they didn't have pacing sticks, so I went out to the woods, and I got a stick, and I made own sign. I put balloons and bunny ears and I was set! I stayed in a Fire Station. There were a lot of cots; I had to use my sleeping bag like the weekend before. There were a lot of hills. It was 89 degrees. I started with a group and I picked up another at the half-way point, and another one at Mile 20. It was a FANTASTIC time!

Hatfield McCoy Marathon

6/17/2017 Niagara Falls International Marathon, USA and Canada

I stayed with Les and Peggy Potapczyk in Canada. When I arrived, I headed to the Expo. I went to Mass on Saturday evening and came home to an enjoyable pasta dinner with wine. The next day, I headed out to the Ultramarathon. It was already extremely hot—it was even hotter than Pittsburgh. Towards the end of the race, I began to slow down, even though I was unofficially pacing another runner. I met him along the course and asked him if he needed help. He gladly accepted my offer to pace him. The aid stations were like oases in the

Niagara Ultra

desert where we poured water over our parched skin. I brought him in the last 6 miles and finished the race with him. As if I hadn't done enough, I instigated a bike ride around the Falls with Les when we got back to their house, logging another 20 miles to the day. When I crossed the finish line, I had no idea what place I had ranked, but to my surprise I received notification in the mail that I was the first place female finisher for my age group!

6/25-27/2017 American Heart Association and Stroke Association

We left Sunday afternoon to drop April, John's dog, at his sister, Marcia's house. On the way, Marcia called and said she was not able to watch April. He made several phone calls to try to get someone to watch his dog, but no luck. So, he came with his dog. Off we went to D.C. April was unbelievable. She is a service dog. We kept her in our room with the "Keep Out"

Washington, DC

John, April, and me in DC

American Heart / Stroke Association DC Group

John's Dog, April

sign on the door. Sunday night we went to the reception at the Stroke Association. Monday morning we broke into groups to discuss how we were going to approach the senators and representatives, and who had what responsibilities. The discussion revolved around current regulations and what changes should be made to benefit the Heart and Stroke Association. People from all over the country were going to meet their US senators and representatives.

I remember when my boys were young and they would watch Schoolhouse Rock "How a Bill is Made." Now I was going to see for myself.

7/1-4/2017 Firecracker Quadzilla, Portland, Oregon

For the Quadzilla, I ran four marathons in four days. I got to Portland, Oregon and took a train to Julia's house. I knew Julia from pacing New York City Marathon. I had stayed with her in New York, and decided to stay with her again in Portland. Her husband, Shane, a new friend of mine, Jennifer Hickey, and I would all be tackling Quadzilla Marathon together, while Julia was running the half-marathon.

As part of my training, I walked to yoga with Julia. Because I was preparing for four days of difficult running, Julia suggested that I go to yoga with her to relax my mind and body. It was invigorating. (Thank you Julia!)

Jennifer Hickey, me and Julia Khvasechko

Foot Traffic Cook Park Medals

The next day, we got up at 4:30 a.m. Julia's house was strategically located 14 miles from each of the four races. Loopy was the first race. The course was only 0.9 miles, but we had to run around the course 28 times. To some people, running around in circles might sound boring, but because I am a people person, it was great! I got to meet a lot of people again and again ...and again... and again... I was so busy entertaining and high fiving that I forgot to run (competitively, that is!) I ended up placing second.

The next race was Cook Park. It was a four mile loop that we had to run six times. The first lap I didn't realize how hilly the course was, but by the last lap, I had to keep telling myself, "I think I can, I think I can..." as I chugged up the hill to the finish.

The third race was Stars and Stripes. This race was 2 loops that were a half marathon each. It was hard. I didn't see nearly as many people as I did during the first race.

The last race of Quadzilla was the Foot Traffic Flat Marathon. There were a whole bunch of people there for this race. I was pacing this race and inviting other runners to run with me throughout the race. Even though it was the fourth and final race of the series, I managed to come out with my personal best for this course, 4:25, which is a Boston qualifying time. This was an amazing feat.

7/22-29/2017 – RAGBRAI "The Register's Annual Bicycle Ride Across lowa"

Chet picked me up in the Chicago airport and brought me to his house. I stayed one night and got to visit with his wife, Kathleen. Chet arranged for me to borrow a high-performance 2016 Trek Lexa Women's bike from an advanced bicyclist, and to my surprise it was the perfect height for me. The next day Chet and I got all of gear for the week (food, drinks, sleeping bag, bike shoes, helmet, all) and loaded it on the truck. Chet and I, along with eight other friends of his from St. Ambrose, drove 5 hours to the rally point in Iowa. We visited over 50 towns along the way and stayed in seven towns. Along with 20,000 other riders, we biked more than 440 miles that week and climbed 12,560 feet!

RAGBRAI AAA Ladies

RAGBRAI Bicycle Arch

Playing Cornhole with Tom Christianson

Tom Christianson, one of Chet's friends, is a retired air force pilot, just like my Dad, and named Tom, just like my younger brother, so I instantly felt a bond. He and I played cornhole and put handprints on the wall in Britt, Iowa.

Hand Prints at RAGBRAI

RABBRAI Volunteers

8/06/17 Drake Well Marathon, Titusville, Pennsylvania

This was the second year I ran this marathon. I had met Bill and Eleneta Ashley at Saint Titus Roman Catholic Church. Reverend Walter E. Parkard introduced me to them and they offered for me to stay with them while I was in town. I stayed with them in 2018 also, for the third year in a row. I got first place in my age group: 4:25! I crossed the finish line, got a plaque and medal, and went the Drake Well Historical Museum and Park. Colonel Edwin L. Drake drilled his well in 1859 and launched the modern oil industry. The site shows how the industry grew

Bill and Eleneta Ashley

as kerosene for lamps and lubrication for Industrial Revolution machinery were refined from Pennsylvania's paraffin-based crude oil. Today, the petroleum industry is global, but it began in little Titusville.

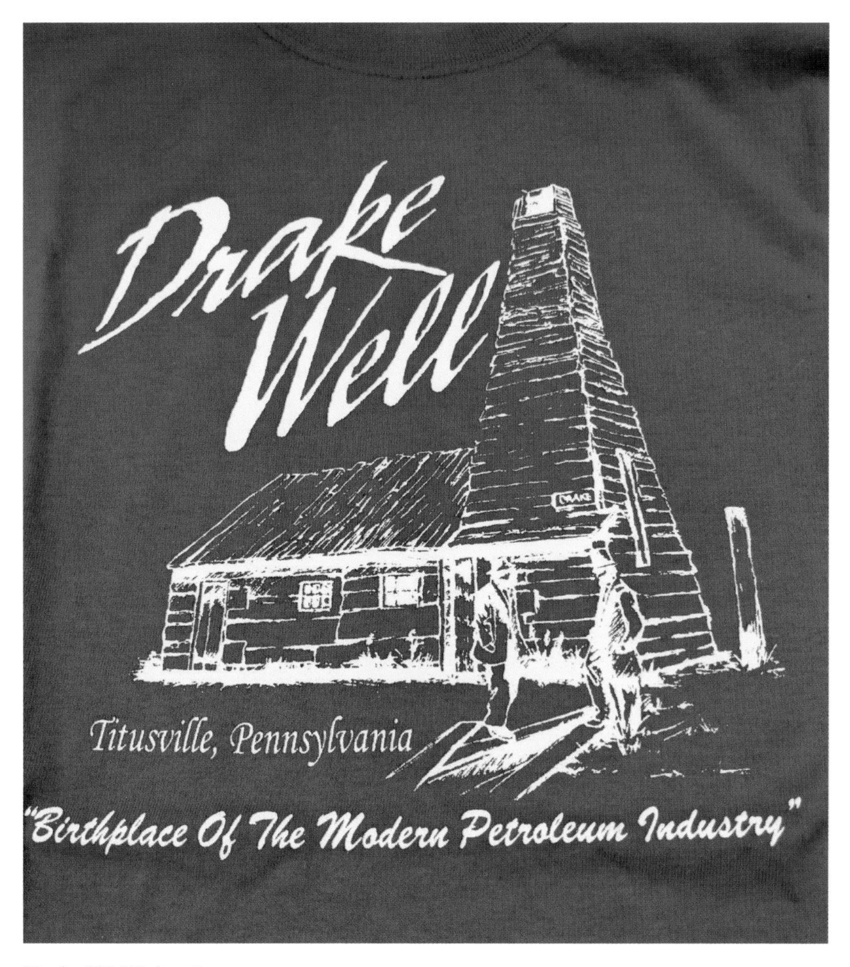

Drake Well Marathon

8/26/2017 Santa Rosa Marathon, California

Beth Carter, the pace leader for this marathon, is a good friend. She lives in Portland, Oregon I had stayed with her and her husband years earlier.

Three years ago, I met Ginger and Maryann, and they gave me one of their skirts. Last year at the Expo, I wore their skirt, and everyone was asking where I got it! I gave them a lot of new customers that day. As a token of appreciation, they gave me a new skirt this year.

The Santa Rosa race was excellent. It was a hot, sunny day. To make it even better, they gave us a bottle of wine at the Expo!

Ginger and Maryann Skirts Designs

Santa Rosa Marathon

9/24/2017 Quad Cities Marathon

Chet Doyle picked me up from the Quad Cities, Moline, Illinois Airport and I went to the Expo. Outside, I ran the kids' marathon. This was my third time running the kids' marathon. Having started the Kids of Steel program in Pittsburgh, it was exhilarating to run with the kids in this race too.

Before the race, I got to see Joe Morino, the race director. I met him long ago, and it was so nice to see him again and get a picture together. Like me, Joe had had a stroke three years earlier.

After the race, I met up with Amy Jo Soeken, an amazing massage therapist. I had met her 4 years earlier. After the race I returned speedily to the tent next to my pace tent to get my much anticipated massage. Amy Jo is a fantastic masseur—my muscles thank you.

I stayed at Chet's house that night, and he took me back to the airport. Off to my next adventure!

Quad City Kids Race

Me, Joe Mareno and Chet Doyle, Quad City Marathon

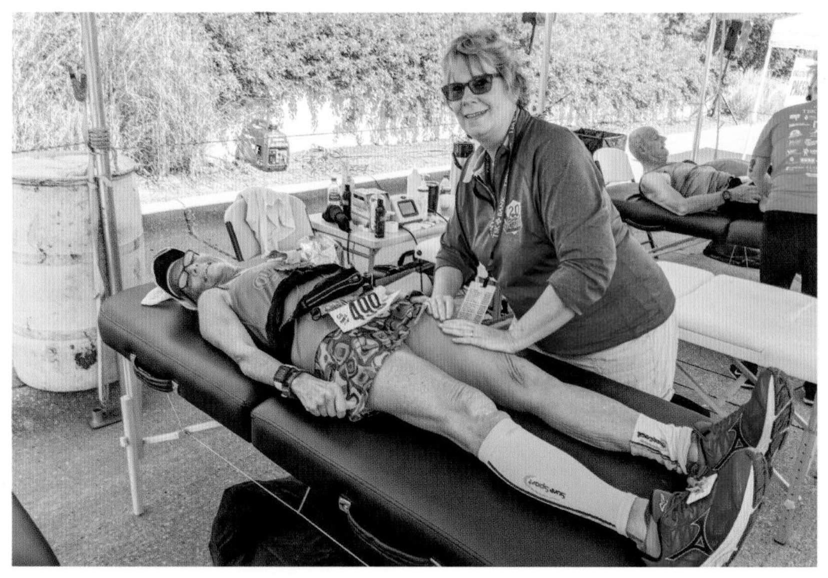

Amy Jo Soeken Massage Therapist.

10/01/2017 Maine Marathon, Portland, Maine

My son, David, and granddaughter, Maddie, picked me up. Spending time with David, Erin and Maddie made the trip extra special. Maine is a gorgeous place to visit in the fall so we took

Maddie Bartoletti and me

David, Erin and Maddie Bartoletti

the opportunity to explore the local fall Festival. Maddie was enamored with the sights of the pumpkins and bales of hay, but no one was expecting to get "caught" in the corn maze. Even though I run marathons practically every week, my legs became tense at the thought of having to double back in the corn maze again and again.

The marathon was Sunday. The route was very hilly, but I had an extra bust of energy from visiting with family which resulted in the ability to conquer the hills and place second in my age

Maddie and me at the airport

group.I stayed with my family until Monday. It's always hard to say goodbye. Tears flowed as we parted at the airport.

10/08/2017 Chicago, Marathon, Illinois

By this time, I had built a strong circle of friends who included Gayle and Janine. We went out to dinner together after the marathon and enjoyed good food and even better company.

Janine, Me and Gayle

10/29/2017 Dublin, Ireland

John and I traveled to the marathon together. We took a bus tour of the city and made a stop at a whiskey distillery for some samples. One stop along the tour that John and I knew we wanted to make was the prison. It's no longer in use, but we saw jail cells and the courtroom. I got in a round of ping-pong with a fellow runner from Marathon Tours, followed by hors d'oeuvres. We also crossed an exquisite bridge shaped like a harp.

After the race, John and I had a photo op with one of the top finishers!

New York City Marathon Pacer 11/05/2017

2017 Dublin Marathon Winner

11/19/2017 Route 66 Marathon, Tulsa, Oklahoma

Cathy and I met in 2008 and we remained friends. She even treated me to dinner the night before the race with her husband and her son. I was elated to see her again in Tulsa. I was pacing a gentle 5:00 which allowed me to have relaxed conversations with fellow runners along the way.

Cathy Ozeroglu and me

12/02/2017 Memphis Marathon, Tennessee

I was pacing 5:00. This marathon is especially dear to John and me. The city comes together for a great cause. The proceeds of the marathon go directly to St. Jude's Hospital. That is why I have paced this marathon for a decade. Mark Vergallito and wife, Darcy, drove down from Pittsburgh (I taught his kids, who were part of the Kids of Steel) I had first talked Mark into a 5K, then a 10K, and a half marathon. Then, I talked him into running this marathon with me. He got the bug to run a marathon and had the Pittsburgh, Chicago, and Niagara Falls Marathons under his belt. The Memphis route was a real tear jerker. As we passed by

Pacing Mark Vergallito at the Memphis Marathon

the hospital, the patients were out there cheering us on. I hugged them and they liked it. We came in together at 4:59:13. You can tell by our smiles that we were proud of our finish time, but even more proud of the good cause.

2018

Thirty marathons and counting including the marathon two days ago in Niagara Falls

2/25/2018 Tokyo Marathon

My body was ready, but mentally, I was scared. I didn't know how I was going to get from the airport to my hotel and back. I didn't know how I was going to get from my hotel to the marathon and back. I didn't even know my roommate! John took me to the Pittsburgh Airport for my 6 a.m. flight with five minutes to spare. My flight made a connection in St. Paul, Minneapolis. I overheard a group of people at the gate who were talking about going to the Tokyo Marathon. I introduced myself and learned that one of these runners had the flu. We boarded the plane for Tokyo, a 12 hour flight. Upon arriving in Tokyo, I learned how accommodating and helpful the Japanese people are! They also appeared to be very germ-conscious as I saw many people wearing surgical masks throughout the airport and in the city. The woman at the information

Museum in Tokyo

booth not only told me where the bus station was, she walked me over to help me buy my limousine bus ticket. I breathed a sigh of relief because things were starting to come to normal. I got out at the Tokyo Hilton, went to my room and found the toilet seat was heated. How luxurious! I'm not going to lie, I visited that bathroom more often than my bladder required. I also found out that my roommate had already checked in. Two hours later, I met up with the rest of the group from Marathon Tours.

The Expo was a two day event. The Marathon Tours bus took off at 9 a.m. for a tour of the city with stops including the Palace, statues of Buddha and a restaurant featuring different types of teas. Every year in mid-May the Sanja Festival is celebrated. We got to see the ornate displays from years past. I saw a shrine where people could offer prayers, and I found this so fulfilling. The bus also stopped to see drummers playing in a band. We each got a chance to drum. That made me feel golden! Next stop was the Expo. We only had an hour and a lot to see.

Saturday morning was the Friendship Run, a 4K run which is more of a pleasure run. I met people from Australia and Ireland, as well as the good ole USA. Bands were playing and the Tokyo race director was on hand. My roommate and I had a photo op with him, complete with our temporary "Tokyo" tattoos! 2K into the event, I was stunned to see a towering Transformer sculpture and paused for a picture. The Gundam robot is over 64 feet tall.

After the Friendship Run festivities, we were all invited to visit a museum. My roommate and I were the only two to take them up on their offer. Two trains later, we arrived. Hundreds of swords and spears were on display. It was like something out of a movie, seeing all of the ancient warriors. Their suits of armor were intricate and the building was full of historical energy.

We left the hotel and walked to the race. My buddies had water bottles and sports drinks, but as we approached the athletes' village, we saw the signs instructing everyone to dump out their bottles. I had been told about this practice the night before at the pasta party, but wondered if it was true. Fortunately, we were

Out of country Medals

Tokyo
Marathoners

offered hydration along the way. That was a first for me in nearly 400 marathons! Another first was the bathroom set up. It was the first time that I had seen designated men's and women's port-a-johns, and much to my disappointment, the toilet seats were not heated like in my hotel room (I paused for a minute to decide if I could hold out for the heated seat, wink wink).

The start line was crowded, and many people wore surgical masks. I took my camera with me, and at Mile 11, I captured a picture of a gorgeous Japanese dragon—a selfie with a dragon!

I added my Tokyo medal to my other continents for a very special display

I crossed the finish line after 4:45 minutes. Overall, the course was excellent and my time in Tokyo was amazing. Each runner was draped in a Tokyo marathon towel at the end. We had to walk another 45 minutes to catch the bus back to the hotel.

On the flight home, I watched five movies and rested. I was glad to be heading home and grateful for my experiences in Tokyo. I called my Mom and John during my four hour layover in Minnesota.

3/04/18 Little Rock Marathon, Arkansas' Race for Every Pace

John and I arrived in Arkansas on Friday. The pacers were staying at the Four Points Sheraton, which was nice, because it was closer to the start line. The hotel shuttle took us to the pre-party, where there were beautiful views of the rivers and delicious food, including pasta and hummus sampler with pita. The drink of the night was "Chariots of Fire" along with wine and beer. From the flight team, to the hotel staff, to the finish line, everyone we met was courteous and kind—not just this particular year, but every year I have run this race. Dave, whose nickname is the "Sexy Canadian", came up to me because he recognized me from the Expo in Fort Lauderdale. In addition to the familiar faces, I met four new people at our table. By 7:30, it was time to leave. But before heading out, I had a photo op with the "Chicks in Charge". Gina and Geneva are among my favorite race directors. John and I worked several shifts at the Expo where we saw pace team leaders

Little Rock Marathon Medieval Theme

Gina Marchese and Geneva Hampton, "Chicks in Charge"

Anthony and Diane, two dear friends. My buddy, Charley, was there, too. Every year he gives me a rock to symbolize "Little Rock." Diane told me Tommie Smith would speak in the auditorium later that afternoon. Tommie, an Olympic Gold medalist who raised a gloved fist during the National Anthem at the 1968 Mexico City Games, wrote the book, "Silent Gesture." After the documentary about Tommie, he rose from the back of the auditorium. We were in awe to see his 6 foot, 5 inch frame making his way to the stage. After listening to his fascinating speech, we had the opportunity to get a picture taken with Tommie. John got an autographed copy of Tommie's book.

Going into races, I try not to have expectations about anything, but I'm always pleasantly surprised at the wonderful experiences that evolve. After that, I was able to run, literally, to evening Mass down the street. At the end of Mass, the priest asked all those running in the marathon to stand and he offered us a special blessing. Donna, my speech therapist, made an adorable outfit for me wear. I had a whole bunch of people who followed. It was raining, they were following me to the finish line! Bravo, bravo, bravo!

3/09/2018 Jerusalem Marathon, Israel

I was part of Team Shalva and had been fundraising for several months. Shalva helps children with disabilities. I dedicated my race to the children of Shalva and in memory of John's dad, who died on December 24, 2017. Chuck took me to the airport and we talked about tennis the whole way because I was going to be coaching at Seton LaSalle.

I got through security and found out there were cancelled flights all over the northeastern seaboard due to a nor'easter. I was depressed and frustrated because I would have to turn around and go home and I didn't have a ride. I went to the airline counter and was told that ALL flights were cancelled and the next possible flight was the following day, the day I was supposed to run! Tears

Jerusalem Marathon Finish Line

rolled down my cheeks and I knew I needed to calm my mind for a minute and get a plan. As I sat in the chair, I texted my contact at Shalva and two hours later, we had a plan! Flights to Washington, DC were not cancelled, so I went from Pittsburgh, to DC, to Zurich, and then Tel Aviv! After waiting in the customs line in Tel Aviv for over an hour, I saw someone holding a "Shalva" sign. I got on the bus and the Shalva director passed out muffins and water, much appreciated!

We had a pre-race party that evening where I picked up my race packet. The rest of the evening was quiet. I left a wakeup call with the hotel and turned in. I woke at 7:00 am and the race was supposed to start at 7:00! I didn't have a thing to eat, grabbed my marathon clothes and headed out the door. I was told that the start of the race was 25 minutes away! I caught a glimpse of the start line between my tears and darted across the street. The Jerusalem marathon is notorious for its hilly, strenuous course. It lived up to its reputation but I didn't have time to dwell on it! I was the only runner at the start line, so I took off. The path for the 10K was clearly marked but when I asked which way to go for the full marathon, no one knew for sure. At a fork in the road, I turned left, but soon found I was supposed to go straight. Eventually, I caught up with a runner who was wearing a blue bib, an indicator that he was in the full marathon. Even though I was distracted, I took pictures of the beautiful sights along the way. The 10K was with me by that point. I helped a fellow runner who was struggling and injured for the last three miles. My friend later remarked to me, "That's what makes pacers 'angels of Mercy'."

My angels included many of my friends, relatives, and anonymous donors who helped me raise the money to fund my Jerusalem Journey. Eddie Koontz was one of those angels. Later I ran into Eddie at the local YMCA pool and was able to thank him in person. I still recognized him even though I taught him when he was only in the 7th grade!

Ed Koontz and me

3/18/2018 Shamrock Marathon, Virginia Beach, Virginia

Stepping back a moment, in 2010 I paced a gentleman named Michael Nicolaides in Richmond, Virginia. Little did I know I taught him how to pace! He invited me to pace 5:30 at Shamrock this year, which was an exciting opportunity. This would mark my 7th time pacing this marathon, Michael's 47th marathon, and my 406th marathon. They had made a course change since my last run in 2014. The course was flat with no turns.

It was a gorgeous day! I went to Mass at the Star of the Sea Church with John on Saturday night. After Mass, every runner got a special blessing.

The day of the race, everything was organized and smooth. I made my pace time even though my watch stopped at Mile 24. Thankfully, my seasoned internal clock kept pace and 5:28:30 was my finish time. We went to the tent after the race. They served excellent stew and beer with a rock-and-roll band playing. There were people dancing, I was one of them! We had the best time. One of my fellow pacers, and a friend of Michael's, was a school teacher. He interviewed me because he said he was was fascinated with me. He would show his students the tape to motivate them to persevere. In addition to the main tent, there was a VIP tent for the pacers with additional food, swag, and heaters. The combination of warmth, full bellies, and beer equaled the perfect snooze environment, but I didn't want to miss any of the festivities.

4/20/2018 Glass City Marathon, Toledo, Ohio

The traditional pasta dinner was held the night before, for all of the local training groups. Jim Poole, the pace team coordinator, asked me in February if I would be interested in speaking. I agreed to speak to a group of approximately 175 runner volunteers. I was so nervous, but John, seated at the front, was able to keep me calm. My speech went off without a hitch, besides the butterflies in my stomach. Afterwards, I got a standing ovation and my butterflies changed to quivers and goose bumps! After dinner, people came up and thanked me, and were amazed at what I had accomplished. The last sentences of my speech were, "When you think you can't do it, think of me. I'm doing it, so you can do it!" I also met three people who ran with me Sunday (I paced 4:45).

5/27/2018 Vermont City Marathon, Burlington, Vermont

Margaret and her friend picked John and me up at the airport and went to the Expo to pick up our bibs. The weekend before at the Cleveland Marathon, my brand new pair of Hoka shoes got completely worn down in that one race. So, at the Expo, I decided to talk to Hoka's manager. He said that they would get me a new pair. This whole weekend was almost completely wasted because I didn't have another pair of shoes. I was feeling apprehensive.

Jillian Duda "Sticks" and me at Vermont Marathon

All day Friday and Saturday I worried that my shoes would not be good enough to race.

On Saturday morning, I went out for a three mile run with the group in my new Hoka shoes, and I knew that I was good for the marathon. I was so appreciative. Their customer service was excellent.

During the morning run, I met Fidel. He saw that I was wearing a triathlon hat, and he said that he wanted to run a triathlon someday. I told him that I'd had a stroke. I wanted to tell him so that he understood why I had trouble talking. He was very accepting.

On Saturday night before the race, John and I were watching television at Margaret's house. There was an interview with Jillian Duda, who would run the marathon the next day. This would be her third marathon, and she had a stroke 17 years ago.

Meb Keflezighi and me at Vermont Marathon

Before the race, I approached Mebrahtom. I'd met him eleven years prior when creating the Kids of Steel group in Pittsburgh. Meb was sad to hear of my stroke. While I was getting a picture with him, I saw Jillian Duda. I introduced myself. She had "Lazy Legs" on her bib and I had "Pacer Marie."

During the marathon, Fidel came to me along with a group of runners who recognized me from last year. Fidel ran by my side for all 26 miles. At the very end, I told him to go ahead and said, "I want to see your butt!" (Pacing can take different motivational skills!) I came in a few minutes after Fidel at 4:59:32.

After the race, John saw Jillian at the finish line. She had finished the race 5 minutes before me, coming in at 4:55. Due to some medical challenges, Jillian needed to have an IV throughout the whole race. Jillian's husband, John, cycled beside her the entire time to carry her IV drip while she ran.

Margaret Ferguson and her father, Carlton, in Fletcher, Vermont

Margaret's boyfriend, Roger, picked us up after the race and took us to her father, Carlton's, house in Fletcher, Vermont, an hour away. We had met twice before.

7/4-8/2018 Firecracker Five, Portland, Oregon

I flew to Portland, Oregon, and rode a train from the airport. Then I walked to Julia's house. Instead of planes, trains, and automobiles I opted for planes, trains, and my own two feet!

Over the next five days, I ran 144 miles. That's five and a half marathons! I received third place for the females overall.

After all the races were done, I took a fantastic yoga class with Julia. After stopping at Julia's house, it was time to head home. As if 144 miles hadn't been enough running, I strapped on my ironman bag, and started the walk back to the train station.

Firecracker Five

5 Marathons in 5 Days

3

Perseverance

Perseverance has brought me through many periods of self-doubt in my life. Was I going to make it through my master's program? Would I become a successful teacher? Was I good enough to coach tennis, track and volleyball? Was I going to be able to help a struggling runner cross the finish line? Each time I met a new challenge in life, I prayed. Prayer has helped to calm and reassure the sensitive, scared part of me.

John has been my rock (and roll) over the years. We've had our share of good times together and tough times too, like when

My Family

I had my stroke. John saved my life that day and has been my dedicated partner every day since. John possess a robust sense of humor. You never quite know what he might say, but he's guaranteed to bring a smile to your face. He keeps me on my toes, as well as in my running and biking shoes. We enjoy our quiet runs and bike rides together as our "us time." Occasionally, we are able to attach some much-needed vacation time to a marathon.

We run the marathon together and relax in the sun afterwards. I love John's family like I love my own, and he is the same way with my family. I love and admire his strength and unwavering commitment.

As I write this is in September, 2018, I have run 101 marathons since my stroke in November, 2015. I like to think of this as a "running total." Get it ? I have logged over 11,000 miles, which is equivalent to running from my house in Pittsburgh, Pennsylvania to Buenas Aires AND BACK! My life continues to be blessed as I recently found out I will have the opportunity to fulfill another of my dreams. I will be completing the Abbott World Marathon Majors in April of 2019. I am thrilled to run in the London Marathon, which will complete 6th major in this series. Not only am I running in London, I am honored to be pacing.

I have been hearing for over 15 years that I should write a book. I kept the book as a "back-burner" idea until I had my stroke. I am typically a very private person. I tend to keep things to myself. Although when I am running a marathon or pacing a marathon, I am the bubbliest person around.

Every runner that I have ever paced has helped me as much (and possibly even more) than I have helped them. The medical professionals who man the medical tents along the race routes are also deserving of my thanks. I don't always catch their names, but I am appreciative of their expertise in keeping me "on the road".

Its hard to look towards the future without looking back at where you've been. My family means the world to me. My parents passed along their faith, their work ethic, and kindness. I am a grateful recipient of those traits. What I do know is that without all these wonderful people, both friends and family, my story wouldn't have nearly been the same. I embrace the joys and challenges of each day as I live my life as a person who had a stroke, a person who loves to run, a person who loves to meet new people, and a person who cherishes the people in her life. Running marathons allows me to be in the present moment. To be in my "zone." To encourage others and share in their excitement as they cross the finish line. With my family by my side, I intend to continue running. I hope to be an inspiration to others who are facing their own challenges in life.

I live by the motto, "With perseverance, you can accomplish anything!" So now you can see the meaning behind the title of my autobiography ***Perseverance***. I hope my story will inspire you to accomplish special things in your life, as well.

With my family by my side, and growing up so quickly, I intend to continue running. There may be a sequel to this book in the future. Stay tuned…